WAS THAT RACIST?

How to Detect, Interrupt, and
Unlearn Bias in Everyday Life

Evelyn R. Carter, PhD

LITTLE, BROWN SPARK

NEW YORK   BOSTON   LONDON

Little, Brown Spark
Hachette Book Group
1290 Avenue of the Americas, New York, NY 10104
littlebrownspark.com

First Edition: January 2026

Little, Brown Spark is an imprint of Little, Brown and Company, a division of Hachette Book Group, Inc. The Little, Brown Spark name and logo are trademarks of Hachette Book Group, Inc.

The publisher is not responsible for websites (or their content) that are not owned by the publisher.

The Hachette Speakers Bureau provides a wide range of authors for speaking events. To find out more, go to hachettespeakersbureau.com or email hachettespeakers@hbgusa.com.

Little, Brown and Company books may be purchased in bulk for business, educational, or promotional use. For information, please contact your local bookseller or the Hachette Book Group Special Markets Department at special.markets@hbgusa.com.

Print book interior designed by Bart Dawson

ISBN 9780316583329
LCCN 2025941848

10 9 8 7 6 5 4 3 2 1

MRQ-T

Printed in Canada

For Martharee & Luther, Lileah & Percy

Contents

WAS
THAT
RACIST?

Introduction

White people and people of color perceive racial bias in fundamentally different ways. And these gaps in bias detection play out in practical scenarios every day. As a Black woman growing up in mostly White environments in the United States, I've amassed a number of experiences where I've felt dismissed and devalued because of my race, only to be ignored when I raised those concerns—told to "grow a thicker skin" by White people who were eager to offer alternative explanations for the racism I *knew* I was experiencing. In my career as a diversity, equity, and inclusion (DEI) professional working in various fields, I've seen what happens when well-meaning White people in positions of power—making decisions about policies and practices that impact people's careers, lives, and well-being—are unaware of the bias they are perpetuating. And while the United States, and the world at large, has seen significant progress toward racial equity in recent decades, it is also undeniable that we're experiencing a powerful backlash, as White supremacy resurfaces in response to strides toward racial equality.

Once, while facilitating a workshop, I was on the *second slide* of my PowerPoint presentation when a White faculty member interrupted me to refute the statement "We all have bias." She insisted that I didn't know her personally and therefore I did not have the standing to speak to whether she did, or did not, have bias. The irony is that her department was at risk for dissolution because of the volume and severity of racial discrimination complaints filed against her and her colleagues. Two things were clear to me in that moment. The first was that, contrary to what she seemed to believe, she— just like all of us—had biases to unpack. The second was that her lack of awareness about that bias was costly—not only for her and her career but for the careers and livelihoods of each and every one of her students.

Many White people are in denial about the degree to which White supremacy still reigns in our society, attributing the reversal of racial progress to political forces, like the popularity of an unabashedly racist president or prime minister. But reducing the persistence and prevalence of racial bias to the influence of a handful of "bad apples" is a mistake, stemming from a lack of awareness of, or a refusal to acknowledge, the deep roots of the racial bias that exists all around us. Of course, this is not the case for *all* White people, but even when I speak with White people who *are* aware of bias, and who *are* working fervently to change their own attitudes and behavior, they tell me how challenging it can be to raise this issue with other White people. They tell me about friends, family members, church members, neighbors, and work colleagues who *just don't get it*. Or they tell me about the people they know who *began* the work to understand and combat bias, only to veer off course because it got too uncomfortable or too demanding or because seemingly competing priorities claimed their attention.

On the other hand, when I speak with people of color, I hear story after story of people who are *tired*. Tired of simultaneously experiencing racial bias *and* shouldering the responsibility of combating it. Tired of being undermined by White people who are unaware of how their own biases and discomfort are impeding racial progress. Tired of having to explain *why* racial equity is a critical component of a functioning society, not a "nice to have" that can be picked up and put down based on the whims of those in power. Tired of being expected to give "grace and space" or the benefit of the doubt to White people who refuse to acknowledge the racial harm they repeatedly do.

The good news is that detecting racial bias is a skill that can be learned, and when White people invest in *building* that skill, meaningful change happens. Over the course of my career, I have seen firsthand the transformation that takes place as White people become more attuned to identifying bias. It ignites a fervor for change that sustains over time— even when things get uncomfortable or demanding or when other priorities emerge. I believe in my core that the only way our world will change for the better is when more and more White people have those kinds of transformative experiences. I suspect that, if you picked up this book, you want to be part of that change. But you may also feel overwhelmed by the scale of the problem, and not sure that there's anything you can do to make a difference. There is *plenty* you can do, and this book is designed to offer a clear path to becoming a champion for equity, helping to reduce bias and foster a more inclusive world.

Conversations about race and racial bias—the very conversations we must have to realize a more just and equitable world—are already incredibly challenging, but they are downright impossible when the people involved don't agree on the same basic set of facts. This is why merely *describing* the gap in racial bias detection has never been enough for me. I want to help White people learn to detect bias in the way that people of color do.

Thankfully, there is plenty of research out there about how to do that, but most of those insights have stayed locked behind the expensive paywalls of peer-reviewed journals and the inaccessible language of academic jargon. Meanwhile, those responsible for steering companies, creating laws and policies, raising children, and shaping our society are without the critical information needed to drive transformation in their lives and the world. And so this book is a guide to seeing the world the way people of color do, to understanding the ways you have been socialized to see (or *not* to see) racial bias, to unlearning those impulses, and to bringing others along on that journey.

As a lifelong lover of research who proudly embraces my inner nerd, I could easily lose myself in discussing the minutiae of this work for hours. This includes dissecting and debating the nuances and merits of different terms—the distinctions between *unconscious bias* and *implicit bias,* for example, or between racial *prejudice* and racial *discrimination* (both of which, by the way, are real conversations I've fervently engaged in, in the past). But it takes only a few experiences of watching someone's eyes glaze over mid-dialogue to realize that these kinds of distinctions—while meaningful in the research world, and somewhat important in a practical sense as well—obscure the real conversation that needs to be had: How do we stop this thing, *whatever* we call it, from happening?

With that disclaimer aside, I *do* need to take a brief detour into the minutiae for one moment. In most places in this book, I have opted to use the phrase "racial bias," which I define as an inclination for or against any racial group that influences how we think, feel, and act toward them. Racial bias is something that anyone of *any* race can have and perpetuate. For example, I, a Black woman, can (and do) harbor racial biases. (This is not a controversial statement or a "big reveal"; as I just said, we *all* have racial biases. This is simply a matter of fact.) Racial bias is also something that can be *directed* toward any race. For example, any person—whether they're White or a person of color—can be on the receiving end of an inclination for or against any racial group. *Racism,* however, is more specific. Racism is what happens when an inclination against a *marginalized* racial group proceeds in a manner that *upholds a system of White supremacy*. That is, whereas racial bias can be perpetuated by anyone of any race *against* anyone of any race, racism is rooted in the need to sustain a social order in which White people and Whiteness dominate. Anyone, of any race, can perpetuate racism (i.e., preserve a hierarchy that prioritizes Whiteness). However, *there is no such thing as racism against White people*. It's a phenomenon that uniquely targets people of color.

Because this book centers on how White people recognize (or fail to recognize) the thoughts, feelings, behaviors, and policies that undermine and disenfranchise people of color, the terms *racial bias* and *racism* could often be used interchangeably throughout. I recognize that reasonable people can, and do, disagree with my perspective here. But I also believe that combating both racism and racial bias is more important than the specific terms used, and that our focus should be on the work to be done—not on the semantics.

Getting better at detecting bias first requires understanding the psychological barriers that White people face when talking about race and racism. For many, this might include embracing the discomfort that comes with the realization of one's bias, and overcoming the fear of being "found out." This is no small feat. *No one* wants to think of themselves as biased—much less be outed as such in public.

The first two chapters of this book will tackle these barriers in turn, identifying the benefits of embracing a growth mindset about racial bias, and acknowledging that while confronting your bias can be scary and uncomfortable, that discomfort is a sign of progress. Once this mindset shift happens, we can begin the real work of breaking down common misconceptions many White people have about the concepts of race and racism. In the subsequent chapters, you'll learn what many White people get wrong about microaggressions, and why White people are quick to find alternative, more benign excuses for these subtle expressions of racial bias when people of color call them out. We'll talk about how being White *is* a racial identity (even if it might not always feel like one), and how the White default—a dominant framework that uses Whiteness and White racial identity as the reference point for virtually everything—reflects a privilege that simultaneously precludes awareness of systemic racism *and* perpetuates it. We'll explore ways to break through that unspoken default to gather new perspectives and build empathy for others.

The last two chapters of the book are a call to action. For true change to happen, simply knowing better is not enough. *Doing* something—by sharing what you've learned with others, by calling out biased statements and behaviors, and by committing to making some sacrifices—is required. I realize these conversations can be daunting, especially for people who aren't used to talking about race and racism. That's why I provide plenty of actionable examples and suggest sample language to help you navigate those pivotal conversations.

The stories and research shared within these pages are meant to inspire you, to challenge you, and to open your mind to new ways of thinking. But I have an important disclaimer—one that I share every time I lead a workshop on bias: Just as no single workshop, however brilliantly designed, can undo the lifetime of socialization that has produced the biases we *all* hold, neither can a single book, however comprehensive or well written. The *only* way to do that is to commit to the consistent, difficult, and rewarding work of challenging yourself to see the world differently *every single day*.

I hope this book becomes one of the tools you use to begin (or to continue) that process, granting you new insights each time you read it. I hope what you learn challenges your thinking, pushes you out of your comfort zone, and encourages you to have conversations with friends, family, and coworkers you might not otherwise. And I hope that it ignites further curiosity about other evidence-based approaches to combating bias.

Finally, I hope that you see yourself and the people you love in the stories shared within these pages. When that happens, I invite you to be vulnerable, to reconsider the things you *thought* you knew to be true, and to be more attentive to the way your behavior affects other people. Above all, my hope is that this book has the power to spark change, transform lives, and contribute to a more just and equitable world.

CHAPTER 1

Growth Mindset and the Practice of Detecting Racial Bias

Growing up, I played the violin—quite well, in fact. At the height of my abilities, I played lengthy concertos from memory, won the highest accolades at state competitions, sat first chair in my high school's orchestra, and successfully auditioned for a seat in the citywide youth orchestra.

I wasn't born with natural musical talent. When I was three years old, my mother taught me a three-step technique that prepared me to play: Hold the violin out at arm's length with the strings facing away from my body, turn my wrist counterclockwise until the strings faced upward, and bring the whole instrument toward the underside of my chin. To call what ensued that day "music" would be incredibly generous, but with time and practice, the shrill cacophony that emerged when I first drew that bow across those strings evolved into something much more beautiful and masterful.

And I practiced *a lot*. I practiced so much that my left forearm—the one I used to hold up my violin—developed a surprisingly noticeable muscle, which amplified the subtle upper-body asymmetry I'd already cultivated from tilting my head perpetually leftward to meet the violin's chin rest. What's more, I had worked my way to a "violin hickey"—the roughened patch of skin on the left side of my neck and on my left collarbone that served as a badge of honor for all my efforts.

But the reason my violin skills developed—and then flourished—wasn't just because I had committed to mastering them but also because I was buoyed by a small but mighty community devoted to my progress. "Make it sing!" became my father's rallying cry as he mimicked playing a violin with a flourish each night as I prepared to practice. As my skills developed, I became my mom's go-to duet partner; she relentlessly encouraged me to rehearse the same passages repeatedly until I mastered them as we played Bach's Concerto for Two Violins in D Minor together. My private instructor ran me through endless drills, gifting me with his undivided attention in every session. Even my younger siblings—who learned to sit through hours-long recitals with something resembling interest—would offer up occasional words of encouragement, which would help motivate me to practice the following day. I jumped at every opportunity to play, even on the days that I *loathed* playing the violin—which happened often enough—because I wasn't alone in my relationship with my instrument. I had a village of people around me, supporting me in pursuit of my skill.

This story would have unfolded very differently if, the first time I drew that violin tentatively toward me and made it screech and wail, I promptly determined that I wasn't cut out to play it, and no one in my family had encouraged me to try again (and again and again). In *that* version of the story—the one in which I refuse to engage in *any* activity that I'm not immediately excellent at, and no one gives me a hard time about it—the violin ends up in our basement, abandoned and joyless, its case collecting dust. Of course, in that story, my conviction that I'll never be able to play the violin becomes a self-fulfilling prophecy.

The idea that a person of *any* age would pick up a violin for the first time and be able to play Bruch's Violin Concerto No. 1 in G Minor with the musicality of Hilary Hahn is laughable. No skill is inherent in us; they are all forged over time.[1] Viewing learning as a journey or a trajectory reflects a growth mindset—the belief that the attributes, traits, and behaviors we have right now aren't fixed, but rather, as psychologist Carol Dweck writes, "just the starting point for development...based on the belief that your basic qualities are things you can cultivate through your efforts."[2] Dweck contrasted this growth mindset to a *fixed* mindset, "a belief that [one's] qualities are carved in stone."[3]

In the decades since Dweck first wrote about these concepts, the goal of cultivating a growth mindset has been embraced by ambitious professionals, managers, seekers of self-help, and students of all ages alike.[4] Countless articles, books, and even songs(!) have been written about the topic.[5] As a culture, we have correctly adopted the belief that a growth mindset helps us all better meet the challenges that come with learning and maintaining any skill. And yet, we have much work to do when it comes to translating this mentality to learning to detect racial bias in ourselves and others. This is due, at least in part, to our misguided understanding of racial bias as an immutable personality trait or a fixed belief system. The fact of the matter is that this ability to detect bias is—like the violin—a skill to be learned.

To be fair, cultivating a growth mindset about racial bias is not as simple as cultivating a growth mindset about other skills. We humans like to perceive ourselves as good, competent people, because perceiving ourselves in this way satisfies two fundamental human needs: the need to be liked and the need to be competent.[6] Many skills—like violin playing—only bump up against one of those needs. If someone is an excruciatingly bad violinist, that fact may threaten their ego a bit, but hobbies are plentiful, and that person's inferior musical abilities will have little impact on whether or not other people like them. But being bad at racial bias detection—that is, the inability to *notice* how we think, feel, and act toward people of another race—threatens *both* human needs. It triggers the fear that we will be exposed for having racial bias (undermining the goal of being liked), while also forcing us to admit that our previous understandings of racial bias were erroneous (undermining the goal of being competent).

This threat is not merely hypothetical. We all want to think of ourselves as good people who don't cause harm to others, so it can be difficult to admit that sometimes we do. But seeing bias as an inborn and immutable trait undermines the truth: Just as none of us is born with a concerto at our fingertips, none of us is born understanding the nuances of how bias manifests. We must be taught to understand its workings. And the stakes are high. A White person who fails to understand their racial bias will harm others by reinforcing the very systems of power and privilege that undermine equity in every facet of our lives. But it's precisely *because* the stakes are so high that we should be motivated to cultivate a greater awareness and understanding of racial bias.

MIND THE AWARENESS GAP

In many ways, these awareness gaps are a product of insidious design. We live and encounter one another in a system that's hard at work to keep us ignorant of both historical and present inequities. For people of color, our lived experiences and the constant threat of racism necessitate frequent and frank conversations. White people, however, lack that same motivating force, and our education system does little to inspire any sense of urgency around understanding racial bias of any kind. For example, when I was in elementary school, I learned about the Pilgrims, who fled oppression in England in favor of freedom in "the New World." If the Indigenous people who already inhabited the Americas were mentioned at all, it was as a mere footnote to the more courageous and compelling White-settler story. There was no mention of the decimation of the Indigenous tribes that followed the Pilgrims' arrival, much less the disenfranchisement and erasure of Indigenous people that continues today. When this past is acknowledged at all, it's often framed in a way that implies it's entirely behind us. Eager to tell a redemptive story of America, and of Whiteness, we fail to acknowledge that little has been done to *earn* that redemption at all.

The system that has kept us all undereducated about both the history of race relations and the present racial dynamics of our society continues to churn out new and increasingly frightening ways to chill bias-detection efforts. An in-depth comparison of social studies textbooks in the states of California and Texas reveals a playbook for the systemic erasure of the truth about the lived experiences of people of color.[7] Unlike its sister textbook in California, for example, a Texas textbook fails to mention that the benefits of the GI Bill—benefits that made the "suburban dream" of the 1950s possible—were inaccessible to many Black veterans due to the discrimination they faced when trying to buy homes. And though both were published by the same company and credit the same authors, only California's textbook notes that post-Reconstruction lynchings were perpetrated to undermine Black political and economic power. Years after reading these textbooks, children who grow up in Texas will have a fundamentally different understanding of race and racism than children who grow up in California do, widening today's partisan divide into a gaping chasm. To reverse this trend, we will all need to become even *more* vigilant about taking responsibility for our own antibias education in the years to come.

THE BENEFITS OF HAVING A GROWTH MINDSET ABOUT RACIAL BIAS

With so much at stake, where to begin? Just as a violinist must commit to early, focused practice to build their technique, we, too, must dedicate ourselves to the continuous, intentional practice of recognizing and addressing bias in ourselves and others. And yet, lingering in the realm of the fundamentals won't be enough to transform a burgeoning musician into a virtuoso. Any great violin player will tell you that musicianship is about more than playing the notes as they're written on the sheet music. It's about the *expression* of those notes—modulating volume, honoring the silences between sounds as integral parts of the piece. Similarly, detecting racial bias is a nuanced art. As the norms that govern our society change, so, too, do expectations about what is or is not okay to say, what is and is not appropriate behavior. (Sometimes, these changes are for the better. Many will likely recall the successful "Think Before You Speak" public service announcements that urged us to eliminate the derogatory "that's so gay" expression from our vernacular.) Context matters, too: What one might comfortably say in a small gathering of close friends might be prohibited from expression at work. In such dynamic environments, you might make an absolute mess of things at the beginning, tripping over your words and uncomfortably fumbling your way through conversations about identity. But as you advance from the fundamentals to more sophisticated ways of understanding bias, you'll one day masterfully navigate conversations about DEI and anti-racism at work, courageously engage family and friends in robust discussions about how systemic racism impacts outcomes in our society, and pursue new opportunities to learn, to challenge their thinking, and to grow.

A GROWTH MINDSET ABOUT BIAS MAKES US MORE OPEN AND CURIOUS

Having a growth mindset about racial bias unlocks our willingness to engage in these behaviors. In a series of studies, Drs. Priyanka Carr, Carol Dweck, and Kristin Pauker found that White participants with a growth mindset about bias (which researchers assessed prior to the study using self-report questionnaires) were more interested in learning about their biases and getting to know people from different racial and ethnic groups than White participants with a fixed mindset were.[8] For example, participants with a growth mindset expressed greater interest in participating in other race-related research studies, engaging in interracial interactions, and completing exercises meant to reduce their prejudice. Although these results were intriguing, the activities participants said they would (or wouldn't) engage in were all hypothetical. To understand how beliefs about bias shaped real-world behaviors—and not just theoretical encounters—would take some researcher finesse.

Any bias researcher will tell you that we often must get creative when setting up our studies. Admitting one's own bias is perceived as a social taboo, so asking direct questions of participants rarely works. People will give the answer they know they're supposed to—"*Of* course *I feel comfortable talking with my Latino colleague! Why* wouldn't *I?*"—which may or may not reflect their true feelings or experience. At the same time, it's difficult to create a situation in a lab setting that mimics the real world while also being controlled enough for researchers to observe the outcome. To navigate this challenge, we look for subtle, unconscious expressions of the concept in action. For example, if I want to *truly* understand how a White person feels when talking to their Latino colleague, I might observe how long they hold eye contact with that person, or track their body language during the dialogue. Fleeting eye contact and crossed arms are both telltale signs of discomfort. While we can control what we explicitly say, our bodies' involuntary movements will always reveal our true feelings.

Physical distance is another proxy for comfort, given the human instinct to keep our distance from the things and people that make us uncomfortable. Carr and her team used this insight to their advantage in a subsequent study, when they gave White participants two chairs and asked them to help set up a room for their imminent conversation with another person. Half of the participants were told their partner would be White, and the other half were told that person would be Black. When researchers measured where participants placed the two chairs, mindset (whether fixed or growth) made no difference—both groups placed their chairs equally close to the chair they believed a White person would soon occupy. The noticeable difference was among White participants who anticipated an encounter with a Black discussion partner: Participants who had a more fixed mindset about bias placed their chairs approximately *nine inches* farther away from their Black partners than participants with more of a growth mindset about bias did. In fact, the growth-mindset participants were prepared to sit just as close to Black conversation partners as they were to White ones, suggesting that they felt just as comfortable about an interracial interaction as a same-race one.

The researchers concluded that the fixed-mindset participants in these two studies sat at a greater distance from their discussion partners because they feared that close proximity would betray evidence—to themselves and to anyone else—of their bias. These participants resemble many White people, who, when asked, overwhelmingly say that their primary goal during interracial interactions is to be liked.[9] It stands to reason that, if likability is the primary goal, and being racist is a decidedly unlikable quality in a person, then wading into the uncertain waters of race- and diversity-related conversations would be incredibly threatening—particularly for those who believe that being racist is an immutable characteristic.[10] With that fear in the back of their minds, it's no wonder that the participants with more fixed mindsets behaved the way they did.

The good news is that it's possible to evolve from a fixed mindset to a growth mindset about bias. In yet another study, Carr and her colleagues demonstrated this by presenting participants with one of two versions of an article that was purportedly published in *Psychology Today*.[11] Both versions featured an anecdote about a person's levels of prejudice over time and described the results of a (fake) ten-year study on prejudice. However, the data featured in the articles, and the conclusions drawn, were different. One article, designed to induce a growth mindset about bias, was called "Prejudice Is Changeable and Can Be Reduced" and emphasized that prejudice can be reduced "with effort and the right experiences." The other article, "Prejudice, Like Plaster, Is Pretty Stable over Time," was intended to engender a fixed mindset about bias and provided the opposite conclusion: that "prejudice, once acquired, is relatively fixed and stable over time." After checking to ensure that they had successfully shaped—at least temporarily—participants' mindsets about bias, they found that participants who had read the fixed-mindset article indeed endorsed more of a fixed mindset about bias compared to those who had read the growth-mindset article. The question, then, was whether this difference in mindset influenced how participants acted in a subsequent conversation. Again, participants were told they would be having a brief conversation with another person who was either White or Black. But unlike in the "chair setup" study, *this* time the interaction occurred. To keep the research environment as carefully constructed yet as realistic as possible, participants were told that the focus of the study was "personal communication" and that they'd be asked to answer some questions about where they were from, to describe a few of their friends, and to offer thoughts on the state of diversity at their university. The conversations were recorded, and researchers reviewed the videos extensively, looking for markers of anxiety (e.g., rigid body posture, speech errors and hesitations, nervous laughter) and assessing for the overall impression of friendliness. They also measured participants' heart rates at various points in the conversation, based on the knowledge that our heart rates increase when we are anxious.

Ultimately, participants who had been induced to have a growth mindset about bias were less anxious and more friendly and had more stable heart rates than participants who had been induced to have a fixed mindset about racial bias—as though believing that they could learn to be less biased gave them permission to be more open and curious. This shift in mindset seemed to reframe moments of discomfort as opportunities for growth rather than proof of personal failure. With curiosity replacing fear, participants approached interracial interactions with greater ease, allowing them to engage more authentically and connect more deeply. As previous studies had demonstrated, having a growth mindset about bias was *so* transformative that it reduced the threat of interracial interactions to the same nonthreatening levels experienced during same-race interactions.

HOW TO CULTIVATE A GROWTH MINDSET
ABOUT RACIAL BIAS

Bias *is* malleable: No one is irreparably racist. Understanding this helps White people feel more comfortable during interracial interactions, and their comfort is generally readily apparent to others. But believing there's room for transformation is only step one. White people who want to go beyond the basics must commit to an ongoing learning process.

During my junior year of high school, I had the opportunity to take Honors Pre-Calculus, an advanced math class that had a bit of a cult following. Soon after the term began, I discovered why kids who survived HPC wore it like a badge of honor: That class was *hard*! Each day I experienced a dull scrambling sensation in my brain as the teacher taught proofs, functions, and calculating probability. I took frenzied, detailed notes and maintained a wide-eyed attention, and still I walked out of each class as confused as I'd been upon arrival—if not more so. But I wasn't one to back down from a challenge, so I marshaled all the resources at my disposal to get me through the course.

My first step was to find a few role models. If other students had survived HPC—and even excelled in it—I needed to know their process. I opted for students who weren't mathematical prodigies (I had little in common with the student who barely needed to study to ace the exams) and came to those conversations with open curiosity and requests for guidance about how to succeed in the course. At the same time, I was fortunate to have a group of friends in high school who were eager to learn about anything and everything that was offered to us. Many of us were in HPC together, and while I tended to study on my own for the other advanced courses we shared, that strategy clearly wasn't going to work in this case. Group study sessions became my default practice. What's more, my teacher offered office hours, and I became a permanent fixture in those sessions.

Importantly, I kept track of my progress. I saved *every* homework assignment, quiz, and test in my pink three-ring binder, documenting evidence that I was indeed seeing improvement, however slight. I don't remember the final grade I earned in that class, though it certainly wasn't an A. But the B– or C+ it likely was meant more to me than every A+ I earned in my high school career. For years, that pink HPC binder became a talisman I'd return to during moments of struggle—a reminder of what I could accomplish with the power of hard work, patience, community, and a belief that growth was possible.

In retrospect, I now see that it was the very belief that I *could* be successful in HPC—even if I wasn't *yet*—that encouraged me to adopt the learning behaviors that fueled my success. It wasn't easy, nor did it always feel good. Studying in a group required a willingness to admit when I didn't understand a concept a classmate was explaining. During office hours, my mistakes were on full display as I worked through problem sets with my teacher. At every juncture, I had to resist the urge to nod and pretend I understood what was in front of me. Leveraging my growth mindset meant trading in that ego-protecting facade for the more vulnerable reality that my knowledge was yet undeveloped and that I needed help.

A growth mindset about racial bias similarly requires shedding an ego-protecting facade and embracing the vulnerability that accompanies a posture of learning. And, just like Honors Pre-Calculus, getting better at detecting bias requires showing up, being curious, finding a community willing to grow together, getting feedback from that community, and working to improve accordingly.

Instead of looking for a role model (after all, none of us is perfect, and there's a near guarantee that the moment you designate someone as a role model, they'll do something cringeworthy or worth correcting), find people modeling the *behaviors* you want to emulate. In everyday settings, this could be the person who speaks up in a meeting after an Asian woman has just been interrupted and says, "Let's let Sarah finish her thought before you jump in." It could be the White parent at the library with an armful of books featuring diverse characters and cultures, or the White person who shows up to brunch with a diverse group of friends and partakes in their revelry at the table beside you. You'll notice these behaviors because they'll make you think, *Wow, I wish I'd thought to say or do that, but I honestly don't know if I'd be that comfortable speaking up like that, or reading those books to my kids, or sitting at that table right now.* Simply acknowledging that discomfort is a step toward growth.

Use those moments of recognition to curate your network. For example, after the meeting, go up to the person who called out the interrupter and ask for a few minutes of their time. Acknowledge your surprise (and perhaps even your awe) that they gave voice to a behavior that you initially didn't even notice. Ask them if they were ever in your shoes, and if so, how they found the courage within themselves to speak up for a colleague. Or strike up a conversation with that parent at the library. As parents, the quest for information about baby gear, pediatricians, and preschools often leads us to initiate somewhat awkward conversations with strangers. Children's literature can be one more such catalyst! Start by asking what made them pull those particular books from the library shelves. Share that you want your child to learn more about all the people and experiences that comprise our world. Ask if they'd share their favorite titles with you.

A network of people with shared values is great. But a *community* that holds one another accountable for learning, and then applying what they've learned, is even better. To the extent that you seek out books like this one, make sure you *actively* read and engage with the content. Highlight and star passages that stand out to you, and make notes in the margins. Then have the courage to connect with others on the same journey and share what you're discovering about yourself. If it feels daunting to do this, remember that one of the best ways to cultivate a growth mindset is to be willing to own up to mistakes and ask for guidance when you need it. It will be uncomfortable at first, but the benefits of this group sharing far outweigh the costs: One person's mistake and the lessons they gleaned from it can serve as a guide, sparing others from the same error.

Finally, learn from your mistakes and track your progress (pink binder or no). When you mess up, pause to notice the impact of what you've said or done. If you ask your Latino coworker, "Where are you from?" and are surprised when his answer is "Tennessee," examine why you assumed he wasn't American. If you stop a Black person in the grocery store to ask where you can find the snack aisle and are met with a confused glance and "I don't work here," ask yourself why you assumed they were an employee and not a fellow patron like yourself. Take in feedback, whether internal or external, and fine-tune your actions for the future. When a similar situation arises in the future and you behave differently, pause and acknowledge that growth, too.

You may not have thought of yourself as racially biased before, but now that you understand the concept of growth mindset, you know that bias is *not* an irreparable indictment of your character and that detecting bias is a skill that can be cultivated over time. Perhaps now you're more willing to acknowledge the biases you have, and—most importantly— you're willing to do something about them. Being the first in your social circle to raise your hand and declare your biases can feel risky. But the only way progress will happen is if more people own their racial missteps and commit to learning from them, ultimately changing their behavior. Here's what that kind of honesty might look like.

I was hiring! A colleague and I were preparing to bring on a research assistant to support our work—a decision that was long overdue. We developed the job description together and pored over applications, carefully crafting a short list of finalists. We were committed to leading an equitable process, so we developed a set of interview questions we would ask every candidate in order to level the playing field (unstructured interviews are a breeding ground for bias).[12] We practiced who would say what to ensure consistency. Finally, we scheduled the meetings and held the interviews with our finalists.

One of our interviews was with a young Asian woman named Christine.[13] The conversation lasted about an hour, and at the end, Christine stood up to shake our hands. I smiled at her warmly and said, "Thank you so much, Robin. We'll be in touch soon!" I can still see the look of horror on the face of my colleague, who explained what I had done shortly after Christine left the room. I think we can all agree that it wouldn't feel great for your interviewer to call you by the wrong name, but my colleague and I knew the more problematic reason behind my name swap: Robin was the *other* young Asian woman who was a finalist in our pool.

One of the ways racism manifests is that individualism is something afforded to White people and not to people of color. However unintentionally, we're often perceived as a monolith—a mass of people with equivalent experiences, characteristics, and belief systems, simply because we share the same skin color. In truth, we have as little in common with others who look like us as we do with any stranger we pass on the street. I've been on the receiving end of the exact same blunder I made with Christine that day, and I know how much it hurts. It's not that I don't want to be identified as Black—I'm *proudly* Black! I'm also proudly an individual, of which my Blackness is only one of many defining attributes. Being seen as "just another Black girl" dismantles who I uniquely am and what I uniquely bring to this world, whittling my dynamic being into a cluster of tired stereotypes. The second I categorized Christine and Robin as "the Asian female candidates," I extinguished their uniqueness, merging the two in my head as some indistinguishable "other."

I realize there's a small chance that sharing that story undermines my credibility as the author of a book on detecting bias. But there's a *greater* chance that you aren't judging me too harshly, because you've likely had a similar misstep. Sharing my own story is a way of admitting that I, too, am biased, while declaring that I'm working to be a little less so, and to do a little less harm, by learning a little bit more every day. In this situation, my growth mindset is precisely what prompted me to pause and think about the impact of my mistake. I reflected on how our brains take shortcuts, like categorizing both women as "the Asian candidates in the hiring pool," and resolved that I needed to work harder to avoid those mental shortcuts in the future (not to mention write down the name of any person I'm meeting with very clearly at the top of my notes!). I also made sure to apologize as soon as possible to Christine, thanking her for her time and acknowledging that my mistake undoubtedly made for a jarring experience at the end of her interview.

Instead of shamefully withholding my mistakes, I'm emboldened by the knowledge that sharing my blunders is an essential part of my growth process. I've observed my own mindful transformation over time, and I know that anyone who is willing to invest the energy and effort (and honesty!) will see the growth and transformation in *themselves*, too. If we hold on to the misconception that bias is fixed and per-manent, rather than seeing it as a fluid and adaptable trait that's available to evolution, we'll give up on the idea of growth altogether—before we even get started.

Learning to detect racial bias is an ongoing process. For as long as we inhabit this world with all our sociocultural con-ditioning, we'll have to keep our ears, eyes, hearts, and minds open for it. This requires exposing ourselves to information that challenges our personal beliefs and worldviews, trying new things and making mistakes—sometimes in private, and other times in the uncomfortable presence of others—and being open to feedback about how what we said or did had a different impact than the one we intended. A person with a fixed mindset would feel threatened by the prospect of all this, but understanding our potential to evolve is the first in a series of steps toward realizing that potential, and all the joys that come with it.

CHAPTER 2

The Gift of Fear

When was the last time you faced the prospect of doing something that really scared you? For me, the experience that comes to mind involves a zip-lining tour on Catalina Island. My mother was in town for her birthday, and to celebrate, my husband and I took her on a day trip to the island. One fact about my mom: She has a surprising enthusiasm for adrenaline-boosting activities (in this respect the apple fell far from the tree), and Catalina's Zip Line Eco Tour is one of the most highly rated attractions on the island. The most exhilarating way my mother could imagine ushering in this next year of her life was, more or less, my worst nightmare: I have a debilitating fear of heights that, despite my best efforts, I've never been able to shake. (Truly. The kiddie roller coasters at most theme parks represent a near-death experience for me.)

But love repeatedly surprises us—sometimes by overriding our most innate terror. I wanted to honor my mother by joining in her joy. And I wanted to challenge myself to experience something new and unfamiliar—even if it filled me with terror. And so, I found myself inquiring about contingency plans as one of the guides fitted a helmet onto my head and strapped me into my harness. If I ultimately decided *against* dangling from a meager rope three hundred feet above a canyon floor, I asked, what was the *very last moment* at which I could reverse my decision? The guide assured me I could back out until the moment my harness was hooked to the zip line, adding that no one had ever reversed course on her watch. *Your solid run of courageous customers might very well be over,* I thought to myself.

We piled into a van that transported us to the top of the mountain, where the first of a series (a *series!*) of zip lines was waiting for us. I watched, stomach churning, as each person in line surrendered to gravity and took flight. Finally, it was my turn. I stepped unsteadily onto the platform as our guide repeated the same safety instructions I'd heard at the bottom of the mountain—though this time, I heard her through an auditory fog. She recommended I take one hand—or even both—off the handlebars so that, spinning freely, I could get a 360-degree view of the canyon during my crossing. Then she clipped my harness onto the line: It was now officially too late to back out. All that was left was for me to step off the platform.

This is the point at which I froze. My mind understood explicitly what I was supposed to do, yet I couldn't align my body with that comprehension. I started racing through my options. Could I beg the guide to unclip me so I could descend the mountain in the comfort of the van and meet my husband and mother—who were currently in flight—at the bottom? Could she just push me over the edge, since every ounce of strength had just drained from my body? My heart was pounding so hard I could feel it in my teeth, my palms were soaked with sweat, and I was no longer inhabiting my own body. *So, this is what panic feels like*, I thought.

Even if your story doesn't entail alarmingly high altitudes, you've likely had internal experiences similar to this: that feeling of a body in disequilibrium, an awareness of the imminent precariousness of life, when running as fast as you can in the opposite direction—or opting out entirely— seems like a perfectly valid, and maybe the only intelligent, option. Panic scrambles our brain in all sorts of ways. The amygdala—the brain's fear center—becomes hyperactive, as does an area of the midbrain responsible for the fight-or-flight response. This makes it hard to think clearly, impacting our memory, our inhibition control, and our attention.[1] And for many White people, talking about racial bias creates that very sense of disequilibrium. No one's life is on the line, per se, but the self-concept—the narrative we tell ourselves of who we are, and the way we present ourselves to the world—certainly might be.

TALKING ABOUT RACIAL BIAS CREATES DISEQUILIBRIUM AND DISCOMFORT

Decades of research has explored why some White people respond in such outsize (and often hostile) ways to interracial interactions and/or conversations about racism. Landmark research conducted by Drs. Jennifer Richeson and Nicole Shelton offers one explanation: that interracial interactions undermine White people's executive functioning, or "brainpower." (For what it's worth, no group leaves interracial interactions psychologically unscathed. In later studies, the same researchers discovered that interracial interactions also drain cognitive functioning for people of color, though for different reasons than they do for White people.[2]) In their 2003 study, White participants completed a series of assessments designed to establish a baseline for each participant's level of anti-Black bias.[3] Then participants were interviewed, by either another White person or a Black person, on two potentially controversial topics: the fraternity systems at their schools, and racial profiling following the September 11 attacks. After this conversation, participants completed a measure of executive functioning called the Stroop task. In the Stroop task, participants are shown a sequence of words—each of which is the name of a color—on a computer screen and are prompted to identify the color of the *text* the word is written in. Researchers can adjust the difficulty of the task by making a color word either congruent with the font color (e.g., the word "PURPLE" displayed in a purple font) or incongruent with the font color (e.g., the word "PURPLE" displayed in an orange font).

In the congruent trials, the Stroop is quite easy—your brain wants to say "purple" both because it recognizes the word *and* because the font color matches the content; there's no competing data in the visual experience. But the *in*congruent trials present a conundrum: Your brain wants to read the word, and it requires cognitive control to override that impulse and instead focus on the color of the font. That's why the Stroop task is such a great measure of brainpower: If a participant can progress quickly through the task—especially on the incongruent rounds—it suggests they possess a great deal of cognitive control. But if they're slower to react to the incongruent trials, or they make more errors in those rounds, it means they're running low on cognitive control.

When Richeson and Shelton analyzed the Stroop results, they found that participants with higher levels of anti-Black bias who'd been interviewed by a Black person were slower to complete the Stroop task than participants with a high level of bias who were interviewed by a White person. Those participants who engaged in an interracial interaction were so focused on controlling, and hiding, their prejudiced impulses from their conversation partner that there was no cognitive energy left over for the Stroop. Conversely, for participants with lower levels of anti-Black bias, there wasn't really an effect to speak of: Whether they were interacting with a White person or a Black person, their brainpower was functioning at comparable levels. In other words, interacting with a Black person drained the cognitive resources of the more biased participants—something they didn't experience when interacting with a White person.

This cognitive toll helps to explain why White people who are uncomfortable during interracial interactions sometimes lose the ability to control their worst impulses, becoming angry, defensive, and argumentative and sometimes attempting to shut down conversations altogether.[4] In her research, Dr. Robin DiAngelo observes that White people routinely use violent language to describe the level of anxiety and discomfort they experience in race-related discussions, indicating feelings of being in psychological danger, and sometimes even in physical danger as well.[5] In *White Women: Everything You Already Know About Your Own Racism and How to Do Better,* Saira Rao and Regina Jackson document a similar pattern of reactions from White women participating in conversations about racism through the authors' organization, Race2Dinner.[6] Whether they recognized it or not, some of these women felt so threatened by the conversations that they continuously redirected their focus—from the harm that racism inflicts on *people of color* to the perceived "harm" that discussing racism causes *White people.* Their brains appeared to short-circuit, reflexively adopting fight-or-flight behaviors such as denial, defensiveness, and diversion.

This research was foundational to both my undergraduate thesis and my later graduate studies. And, as a Black woman who grew up in largely White spaces, my lived experience gave me further insight into how White people react when they experience acute anxiety during an interracial encounter. Yet nothing prepared me for my first experience with how much White discomfort could hamper DEI progress within a corporate space.

It was February 2020, and I was working with one of my long-term clients on the next iteration of our partnership, having spent the previous year leading unconscious-bias workshops for their global organization of approximately five thousand employees. This was a tech company with employee demographics quite familiar to me—mostly male, mostly White and East Asian—and I'd observed the consequences of this nearly blanket homogeneity during our workshops. After two hours of dynamic and meaningful dialogues about strategies attendees could use to mitigate their own personal biases, the one or two Black people in attendance would inevitably approach me, thank me for my work, and ask with skepticism in their voices but pleading in their eyes: "What will happen next?"

I'd share my genuine hope for their organization's continued transformation. Their employer was doing the work, I assured them. And they were! The unconscious bias education rollout had gone incredibly well, helping employees understand the negative impact of their biases, racial and otherwise. Questions had shifted from "How do you know I'm biased? I'm a caring person," to the more self-aware "I think I've committed a microaggression. What do I do now?" Employees were genuinely eager to know what actions they could take to foster a more inclusive environment, and company leadership seemed committed to this next chapter in our partnership, which we agreed would involve my working with the company's Learning and Development team and its newly hired DEI executive to develop workshop content on allyship that would suit their learning goals. I drafted a project plan like the one we'd used for previous work together: two to three rounds of content revisions, pilot sessions, and a cascading delivery plan beginning with the executive team. We got approval from the stakeholders involved and set a generous timeline for the workshop launch at the end of April.

A few weeks into development, it became clear that this project would be anything but typical. For one thing, the list of stakeholders involved began to balloon. Every few days, my client contacts would send me the name of yet *another* leader who wanted to preview the deck we planned to use. Through several hour-long meetings, groups of people I had never met pored over the deck slide by slide, requesting wording changes on each one. I was asked to craft as close to a verbatim script as possible, and when the newly involved stakeholders learned that workshop facilitators typically shared personal stories, I was asked to collect them for advance approval.

Eventually, whole sections of the workshop were up for discussion. Stakeholders were worried that the concept of privilege—a special right, advantage, or immunity granted to a person or group because of their identity—would alienate White people and suggested we omit the topic. Given that allyship is *specifically about* how people need to use their privilege to foster equity, this was impossible, I explained, as clearly and kindly as I could, using plenty of research and case studies to back myself up. But no level of detail, explanation, or empirical justification seemed to be enough. I stood by while people who were neither DEI subject matter experts nor facilitators in any regard modified the content beyond recognition.

After weeks of meetings, back-and-forth emails, and postponed start dates of the rollout, my partners on the DEI team came back to me. They were flabbergasted and apologetic for all the hoops I had been asked to jump through already. With deep, tired breaths, they let me know of one more coming my way. The chief human resources officer—a White woman to whom the DEI leader reported—wanted to meet. She and other company leaders were apprehensive about making White employees uncomfortable during the workshop. Instead of scheduling another meeting, she proposed that the most effective way to secure final approval from the leaders was through the company's usual method for presenting ideas: a memo. (Never mind that in eighteen months of working with this client, the word "memo" had never emerged from *any* of my collaborators' mouths.)

So, in April of 2020, I drafted an eight-page single-spaced memo for the company's executives. It traced the DEI journey their organization had been on and highlighted my company's involvement in guiding this transformation. It connected the organization's public-facing values—values established by some of the *very* people I was writing to—to the themes of the proposed allyship workshop. It even identified how the "values in action" behaviors that were embedded in employee messaging from onboarding onward would be underscored in the workshop. I summarized the research (some of which I had personally conducted) that informed the content of the workshop; I also emphasized how thoughtfully we designed the workshop's flow to build trust and psychological safety for attendees—even as they might grapple with discomfort. I noted that centering White comfort at the expense of a real discussion about the impact of bias on people from marginalized groups was exactly what the allyship workshop was designed to prevent.

It was difficult to translate everything I would typically say in a real-time dialogue into a written document—a difficulty compounded by the fact that neither I nor the DEI leader would be in the room as the topic was discussed among leadership. The chief HR officer was the only person with enough context to answer any questions that might be raised, and—we hoped—to advocate for this work. We set a new launch date for the last week of May and crossed our fingers that the memo would sway minds (and maybe even touch a heartstring). But after a too-brief interim came a reply: The company's leaders wanted more time to "get comfortable" with the idea of the content (comfort, I was beginning to believe, was one of the company's *real* core values), and they asked us to postpone the launch—again—until the end of June.

I felt thoroughly defeated. I had employed and exhausted every tool I had access to at that time—pulling in research from a variety of sources to convince leaders who were sticklers about data, demonstrating my commitment to our partnership, and leaning on colleagues to brainstorm creative solutions. I had even invited my boss to join in on a few calls to ensure I was communicating clearly and not defensively. When I wasn't actively working, I was turning this client over in my mind, wondering how I could approach the leadership team differently to get them on board. I fielded grateful, kindhearted, and thoughtfully apologetic emails from my client partners, who assured me there was nothing I could've done more or differently in the face of such unyielding desire for White employee comfort. Nevertheless, the whole process had taken a toll: I'd begun doubting myself and my ability to be an effective consultant.

And then, on May 25, 2020, George Floyd was murdered. Within a week, I was invited to a meeting with the core team of internal partners and the chief HR officer—the same White woman partially responsible for the series of delays we had faced. With tears streaming down her face, she apologized for what she now realized were needless, insensitive barriers she'd erected between our workshop and her organization. She acknowledged her responsibility and her culpability, repentant that it had taken a man's murder to see these things in herself. She committed herself to defending our work and ensuring we could move forward. Days later, I received another email. Not only was the client ready to launch on our established June date, but they also hoped we could start the sessions sooner.

I generally cringe when I hear people talk about the "racial reckoning" of the summer of 2020. People point to George Floyd's murder as a turning point—as the moment America "woke up" to the racial injustice and anti-Blackness that's so deeply ingrained in our national DNA, failing to acknowledge that many of us were *quite* awake to this injustice already. And yet, working as a DEI consultant throughout that summer, I witnessed firsthand just how transformative that pivotal moment was for some people.

For years, I'd heard—and on occasion had genuinely repeated—the message that "DEI work takes time" and that "real change is slow." On the one hand, I stand by this senti-ment. Racism has had a centuries-long head start compared to modern-day interventions to combat inequity. Moreover, progress is not linear—historically, every major advancement in racial equity has been met with a swift and severe level of backlash.[7] The barriers we must dismantle to achieve last-ing racial equity are substantial. With this frame of mind, I'd told myself that the leaders of my tech company client *were* committed to their DEI efforts; this was simply what "slow" progress looked like. And then George Floyd was murdered—and suddenly change started happening *very quickly.*

I realized I had been wrong in my initial assessment of these leaders. They weren't slowly but diligently working toward dismantling mountainous barriers to equity and justice. There was no growth mindset about bias in this group. If anything, they were creating *new* barriers by convincing themselves that their discomfort was an accurate litmus test for whether the work should continue. Like the White participants whose brains and bodies felt the warning signs of panic during the one-on-one conversation with a Black interviewer, the leaders of my client were displaying telltale signs of racial anxiety—at scale. Perhaps even worse, they were doing so while convincing themselves they were doing their due diligence.

Until, that is, a Black man was murdered, and corporate America could no longer avoid taking the very actions on DEI that they should've taken long ago, lest they be taken to task on social media. But as the summer drew on, that bitter but momentous twenty-fifth of May became the fulcrum of so much of my inquiry. What was it about George Floyd's murder that motivated grand-scale action so swiftly? (It's not as if George Floyd was the first Black man to have been murdered by police.) Or rather, what had been missing prior to his murder that kept no small percentage of Americans "sleeping"?

Return with me to Catalina Island—because I think my zip-lining experience offers some insight that helps answer those questions.

FINDING YOUR "WHY"

Back on Catalina Island, as I shuddered and sweated on that platform, trying to overcome my fear of gravity, something astonishing happened: I began to come back to myself, to reinhabit my own body. Through the fog of diminishing panic, I could see how all the "outs" I was giving myself were ways of skirting the truth of immediate experience. Like the executives who postponed our allyship workshop, I was delaying action because I was uncomfortable and afraid. And so I grounded myself in a simple statement of fact, followed by a question: *Something in me already agreed to this. What did* that *version of me know that I can't quite see in this moment?*

That's when it dawned on me—I hadn't committed to this nerve-wracking, disorienting challenge in order to make my mother or my husband proud. I wanted to be proud of *myself* for facing my fear. I wanted to be able to look at myself in the mirror afterward and say decisively, "Evelyn, you did a really hard and scary thing today. A remarkable thing, even. And I see you and celebrate you for what you've done." This realization—that I was doing the hard thing for myself—was what finally made it possible to take a deep breath, squeeze my eyes shut, and step off that platform.

I was able to take that leap, in other words, because my motivation for doing so was intrinsic—it came from within me—rather than extrinsic, which would have been driven by outside pressures telling me it was important. To be sure, my mom's birthday wish was the external catalyzing force that initially prompted me to say yes to the activity, but the reason I was able to follow through was because conquering this fear was personally important to me. And as the research demonstrates, people are more likely to adopt and sustain new behaviors—even uncomfortable ones—when they're motivated from within.[8] In contrast, *extrinsic* motivation may lead to temporary behavior change, but it tends to diminish quickly—especially when challenges arise. For those driven by external motivation, discomfort often triggers a desire to flee or react defensively, convincing them that the issue lies with the situation, not in themselves.

There are any number of reasons why White people may become motivated to increase their awareness of racial bias. Perhaps it's a push from a loving friend or family member, the obligation to participate in a company's DEI training session, or a desire to keep up appearances in the "anti-racist book club" they were invited to join. These extrinsic motivators can certainly be helpful for getting people through the door. Once inside, however, they'll likely discover that the path ahead is long and hard—that the two-hour workshop

Was That Racist?

on unconscious bias is a *start*, not the end of the journey. And without *intrinsic* motivation to accompany their efforts, they'll soon get off the train. They'll stop participating in the DEI programs at work, lose track of their initial enthusiasm for dismantling bias, and slip back into "business as usual."

INTRINSIC MOTIVATION AS THE
KEY TO LASTING CHANGE

To engage in the difficult, ongoing process of identifying and challenging racial bias, you must discover what makes that work personally meaningful to you. Maybe the friend who urged you to reconsider your views on bias shared an article that appealed to your sense of justice, or the facilitator of that training told a story that sparked empathy for people with experiences different from yours. Whatever it is, once the intrinsic motivation kicks in, detecting bias is no longer a means to an end; it's about the genuine desire to make the world a better place. If you find that you are typically unmoored by race-related conversations, intrinsic motivation is the antidote to that discomfort.[9]

Drawing on more than thirty years of research on the "self-regulation of prejudice," Dr. Margo Monteith identifies intrinsic motivation as the crucial factor that determines whether people are willing to examine and alter their biases.[10] When an extrinsically motivated person does something biased—clutching their purse tightly and crossing the street when a Black man approaches, or confusing the names of their two Indian colleagues—their primary concern will be whether other people caught their blunder. If it goes unnoticed, they're likely to brush it off and proceed without a second thought. In the event that other people *did* witness their behavior, extrinsically motivated people will justify it: Defensive excuses surge to the tips of their tongues and often emerge in a mess of fiery language.

Intrinsically motivated people take a different approach. Instead of giving in to that defensive impulse, they're able to view the mistake as an opportunity to pause and notice the impact of their behavior. That is, instead of lashing out at someone else for pointing out their mistake, intrinsically motivated people feel disappointed, guilty, or ashamed *with themselves*. They interpret their sweaty palms and that unsettled feeling in the pit of their stomach as signs that their behavior did not align with their values. They can acknowledge, *Who I was just now is not who I want to be*, allow themselves to feel the full weight of their negative emotions and discomfort, and turn those emotions inward. This mindful processing paves the way for consciously developing new habits that take the place of the behaviors they wish to change. The next time they're walking on the street and a Black man approaches, their brain sends out a little reminder signal that says, "Remember last time, when you got this wrong? Remember how awful it felt? Don't repeat that same mistake." Then, instead of clutching their purse and crossing the street, they make eye contact with the Black man and smile. Over time, "make eye contact and smile" replaces the "clutch my purse and cross the street" instinct, with the latter becoming a distant memory of how they used to behave.

DISTINGUISHING BETWEEN INTRINSIC AND EXTRINSIC MOTIVATORS

On the proverbial zip-lining platform of anti-racism, extrinsically motivated people and organizations turn around, get back in the van, and head comfortably back down the mountain. But *intrinsically* motivated people and organizations treat discomfort as a call to action—a sign that they're closer to aligning their behavior with their personal values. Still, I try not to judge people who approach DEI efforts from a place of extrinsic motivation. We all have some kind of starting place, and *whatever* motivates someone—whether it's from within or without—gives me fodder to work with.

In hindsight, I should've understood that my 2020 client was primarily motivated by external factors. The driving force behind the "good work" I'd observed wasn't rooted in personal or organizational values. Instead, it stemmed from a desire to avoid negative press over the inequitable attrition of Black employees, or to stay competitive with peers who were investing in DEI. By early 2020, unconscious bias had become so embedded in our cultural conversation that company leaders didn't object to that workshop topic. But allyship was a new frontier reserved for "social justice warriors" and others perceived as being at the fringe of society; the external pressure on the company's leaders wasn't strong, prominent, or persuasive enough to drive sustained commitment. But that changed radically after George Floyd was murdered. Suddenly, caring about racism and engaging with more sophisticated DEI topics like allyship was not only important but also fashionable. And so, after months of postponing and prevaricating, my allyship workshop was a go.

That client experience fundamentally shaped the way I engaged as a DEI practitioner. Had I realized, back in 2020, that the company I was working with was an extrinsically motivated organization, I might have taken a different approach to working with them. Instead of internalizing their resistance as my own failure, I would have understood it as the behavior of an organization driven by external influences. My attempts to spur them to action would *not* have focused on telling the story of the company's DEI journey and progress, positioning allyship as the next logical step on that journey; and I wouldn't have drawn upon their company's values and employee impact stories to build a compelling case for allyship: *"You said you wanted to become a more inclusive company, and look how much progress you've made. Trust me to take you through the next phase."* For an intrinsically motivated group armed with a growth mindset about bias, that opportunity to reflect on their progress would likely have been enough. But the tech company I was working with would likely have been more receptive to a different message: *"In every other area, you aim to lead, but in this space, you're lagging behind your competitors. Eventually you'll be too far behind to remain competitive for talent and market share. Is that what you want?"*

From that time onward, before agreeing to work with an organization, I did my own due diligence to understand the motivations behind the requested DEI work. I reviewed the company's values and demographics. I asked about the investment—time, money, or other resources—they would be willing to provide. The information I gathered in this process helped me understand what was driving this company to embark on their DEI journey and to adjust my approach accordingly.

The success of my workshops has consistently been strongest with organizations whose underlying motivation—their "why"—comes from intrinsic values. In many cases, the company's leadership is discouraged by the lack of representation of people of color and the persistently low engagement scores from the employees of color they *do* have. I've spoken with many a startup founder who'd dreamed of creating a diverse and inclusive company that treated *all* people equitably, and their struggle to realize that utopia was what motivated their request for help. For those organizations that had already bought in, I could jump right into a discussion about the impact of bias, how inclusive cultures benefit all employees, and tactics to cultivate inclusion and address bias individually and systemically.

Other times, the goals I heard about were rooted in extrinsic motivation: A company leader wanted to remain competitive in the market (there's no clearer example of an extrinsic motivator for addressing racism than the statement "I want my company to make more money"), or they were afraid of getting bad PR and knew DEI training could help assuage angry employees and consumers. *Those* organizations still needed to hear about the impact of bias and the importance of inclusive cultures, but I knew I'd have to begin the conversation from a more business-oriented perspective— one that acknowledged bias as a barrier to output and productivity, preventing both employees and the company from achieving their full potential. Then, with my foot firmly in the door, I'd be able to begin the real, transformative work.

For individuals, I took a similar approach, asking a variation of the question I'd asked myself on that zip-lining platform: *"Something in you already agreed to this. Why?"* In workshops, I'd ask why behavior change mattered to them; in coaching sessions, I'd explore what motivated them to seek guidance on this topic. Participants shared a wide array of answers during these discussions. For some, admonishment from people they care about had shocked them into an awareness of their biases. For example, immediately following George Floyd's murder, I fielded call after call from White parents who were perplexed, hurt, and confused that their teenage children were calling them racist. They didn't see themselves that way, but their kids' approval was so important to them that they knew they had to take the accusations seriously. For others, their motivation came from within, spurred by a desire to live in closer alignment with the values that governed their behavior in other areas of their life. For example, some of my favorite conversations were with people whose religious beliefs motivated them to raise their own awareness of bias and call others to do the same. The ubiquity of news coverage about George Floyd's murder and the persistence of racism prompted them to view the world around them through a new lens and to apply the teachings of their religion—loving and caring for others, making the world a better place—to a broader swath of issues. As a result, they came to understand social justice as central to their religious calling: to confront, not compound, the injustices of the world. Hearing the intrinsic motivations behind people's commitments helped restore some of the faith in humanity that I had lost that summer. Even better, I watched the individual transformations lead to ripple effects within the workplaces and communities they were a part of.

I still believe that meaningful change sometimes *does* take time; progress can be slow, and the process is not always pretty. Case in point: I made *quite* a scene on my first zip-line ride. I screamed my lungs out the entire time, and I *definitely* held on to the handles as tightly as possible with both hands. But I was pleasantly surprised to learn that the remaining rides got successively easier. Afterward, I even (genuinely) smiled for a group picture.

Acknowledging our biases can be similarly daunting. Luckily, a growth mindset has both patience and compassion at its core, and intrinsic motivation helps us build the resilience required to sit in the discomfort long enough for behavior change to occur. In my experience, getting individuals and organizations to identify, and ground themselves in, their "why" for doing this work is often the part that takes the most time. But once that happens, we can surrender to the fear and take that all-important step off the metaphorical platform.

CHAPTER 3

Racial Bias
Can Be Subtle

At my midwestern middle school, the eighth-grade class trip to Washington, DC, was a significant rite of passage. Eighth grade was the year the students at Columbus Academy took a class called Civics, and the end-of-year trip was a kind of culmination: our opportunity to experience firsthand everything we had read about in our textbooks. The multiday itinerary was jam-packed, beginning with a stop in Gettysburg, Pennsylvania, on our way to DC, where we had a stop scheduled at the National Mall for photo ops at select monuments and tours at the Smithsonian and the Holocaust Memorial Museum,[1] followed by an excursion to the Capitol Building. At the time, nothing sounded more exciting to me.

My friends and I prepared for the trip by scrutinizing our packing lists, lobbying our parents for spending money, and—in my case—getting my hair done. At the time, my thick, shoulder-length hair was in its fully natural kinky-coily state. At home, I had all the tools and products needed to style it to my heart's content, but my limited luggage capacity meant some hairstyling accoutrements would have to remain behind. Besides, hair can be quite unpredictable: While there were days that I could style my hair to my own satisfaction in less than ten minutes, on other days it would take a full hour. For this extended trip, I needed a style that would require little maintenance *and* be super cute. Cornrows were the perfect solution. I got my hair done the day before our departure, and the following morning, giddy with excitement, my hair tucked away into braided buns, I was ready to go.

As I stood in the school parking lot with my friends, waiting for our buses to arrive, one of them commented on my hair. She led with a compliment and then asked, "How are you going to wash it when it's braided like that?" I explained that I wouldn't—I typically only washed my hair every two weeks anyway, so the braids would stay put until then.

"Ew."

My friend with straight strawberry-blond hair wrinkled her nose as she recoiled ever so slightly. She then explained that her hair would become an oily mess if she waited that long between washes. The other girls in the group nodded— the same was true for them, and they were baffled that it wasn't the case for me. I had always been vaguely aware of the fact that I was the only Black girl in this group of friends at school, but this was one of those occasional moments when a single word or gesture drew an invisible but abrupt line through the group, separating me from everyone else. Stinging in the wake of her reaction, I went into educator mode as I explained that my hair was materially different from theirs. That, in fact, I needed to retain some oil in my hair and on my scalp, and so frequent washing would hurt more than it would help. After a chorus of "ohs," the conversation among my friends turned to the next topic. But while they had moved on, I remained spinning and disoriented.

When my friend uttered that single, consequential syllable—"ew"—she hadn't intended it as a comment about my race. And yet, I *knew* it was. Whenever I was with my Black friends, many of whom also wore cornrows or other long-lasting braided styles, our conversations about hairstyling often centered on the shared dread of the hours-long process of "wash day." They would never be disgusted to learn I didn't wash my hair for days at a time because they didn't either. This was our reality. But to my White friends, who were used to their own reality being the default, anything different was an outlier experience that demanded an explanation. To them, my hair-washing habits were more than just different. They were gross, weird, and wrong. And in the moment of that "ew," I, too, felt worse than different. I felt gross. I felt weird. I felt wrong.

RACIAL BIAS IS BIGGER THAN
"THE N-WORD"

I think most of us would agree that "ew" is an insensitive response to offer a friend under *any* circumstances—but, you may be wondering, was this *really* an example of racial bias? To which I say: great question. Recall that our working definition of racial bias is "an inclination for or against any racial group that influences how we think, feel, and act toward them." Through the lens of this definition, the answer is *yes*. The visible recoil signaled an inclination against Black people (as represented by my "Black hair"), and it shaped how my friend viewed, felt about, and responded to me ("ew").

I've observed that the race of the person I'm sharing my middle-school anecdote with is often what shapes their response. When I share this story with other people of color, they nod, roll their eyes, and recount their *own* stories of that painfully drawn invisible line. But when I share it with White people—particularly those who haven't yet honed their racial-bias-detection skills—I often encounter skepticism. Responses include: "That was unkind, but not *everything* is about race"; "It doesn't sound to me like she meant to hurt you"; or—my personal favorite—"It's not like she said the N-word or anything, Evelyn." Rather than honoring my lived experience and the bias I identified in our pre–Civics adventure conversation, White people typically put a great deal of effort into convincing me that my interpretation is erroneous.

It must be said: "Not using the N-word" is an incredibly low bar to use when determining whether someone's words or actions betray bias. What's more, whether my friend meant to hurt me is beside the point, and focusing on whether or not she intended to cause harm discounts the negative impact her words and gestures actually had on me. Unfortunately, this narrow definition of how racial bias manifests—the idea that *real* bias is blatant and malicious, and anything less than that isn't really bias—is one that White people typically default to. Perhaps unsurprisingly, it's quite different from the more expansive definition of bias that people of color use: one in which bias can be subtle—and even well-intentioned.

Indeed, research reveals that Black and White people often define racism differently.[2] In one study, Drs. Sam Sommers and Michael Norton asked a racially diverse group of participants to consider the term *White racist* and, based on their experiences and perceptions of this category of person, list up to five behaviors associated with it. The resulting list included twenty-nine different behaviors, such as *belongs to a group that promotes racial bigotry, thinks slavery happened so long ago that it is unimportant to talk about,* and *only has White friends.* Then the researchers asked *another* racially diverse group to indicate how much they believed each of those twenty-nine behaviors was indicative of racism—essentially, Sommers and Norton wanted to know how "quintessentially racist" each of the behaviors appeared to the second group. Finally, the researchers used statistical analysis to sort the behaviors into three categories: "overt racism," "denying racism," and "discomfort and/or unfamiliarity with Black people." The "overt racism" category included behaviors like *denies group membership to Blacks on account of race, belongs to a group that promotes racial bigotry,* and *discourages kids from playing with Blacks.* "Denying racism" comprised behaviors such as *believes that prejudice against Blacks is no longer a problem* and *thinks slavery happened so long ago that it is unimportant to talk about.* And "discomfort and/or unfamiliarity with Black people" included behaviors such as *feels anxious around Blacks, only has White friends,* and *laughs at another person's jokes about Black people.*

More interesting than the themes themselves, however, were the racial group differences that emerged. *All* participants, regardless of race, agreed that behaviors in the "overt racism" and "denying racism" categories were equally indicative of racism. However, White participants were far less likely than people of color to agree that behaviors related to "discomfort and/or unfamiliarity with Black people" constituted racism. This third category captured a subtler way that racism can manifest—with behaviors that might plausibly be attributed to something other than racism (and often *are,* by White people), but that people of color would attribute (as they did in this study) to racism.

The obvious reason that White people tend to gravitate toward an overt definition of bias is because those open, undisguised behaviors are easier to identify. But I suspect it runs deeper than that. I believe the distinction many White people draw between biased behavior and not-biased behavior is rooted in a desire to make intention (rather than impact) the distinguishing factor. It's true, there's a significant difference between someone who can't help but feel a little uncomfortable around Black people and someone who chooses to join a hate group like the KKK. However, the challenge with focusing on intent is that it leaves little room for the impact that bias has on its recipients. All biased behaviors—whether it's making a passing judgment about a young Black girl's hair-washing habits or marching with a Confederate flag in a Black Lives Matter counterrally—have some degree of negative impact. And all biased behaviors—not just the ones associated with being a literal card-carrying racist—demand accountability, reflection, and change. Relying on an overly narrow definition of racial bias—one in which only the most overt behaviors count—creates a wide berth of absolution that allows White people to continue doing harm without having to reconcile their behavior with its impact.

Detecting subtle bias requires cultivating the skills to decipher the impact our words and behaviors have on others. And doing that requires understanding *why* people of color see racism the way we do.

THE COGNITIVE COST OF DETECTING SUBTLE BIAS

Over the last several decades, societal norms have shifted such that overt expressions of racial bias are generally perceived as improper, wrongful, or taboo.[3] But this doesn't mean that bias has disappeared; rather, the way it's expressed has changed with the times.[4] The shop owner may have removed the "Whites Only" sign from the storefront door, but they now direct their employees to "keep a close eye on" non-White patrons who enter the shop. Hiring managers may no longer outright reject candidates based on race, but they now justify favoring White candidates over Black ones by citing concerns about "lowering the bar."[5]

While these subtler manifestations of bias may *seem* relatively harmless compared to the more overt expressions, they are, in many ways, much more harmful—precisely *because* they're insidiously hiding in plain sight. Overtly racist store signs, hiring practices, and policies are unambiguous and easy to spot, but subtler ones take energy and effort to identify.

The store clerk might, at any time, perceive our actions as suspicious, leading to an intervention by mall security or the police. To avoid the risk of such an interaction, people of color might choose not to shop at the store at all. Similarly, the Black person perceived as "subpar talent" by their manager will be more closely scrutinized and held to a higher standard than their peers, only to be overlooked for promotions and performance bonuses. Rather than enduring that ordeal, they may instead be carefully listening for leaders who demonstrate the genuine belief that diversity is a strength, not a concession: *That's* the company they'll choose to work for. In other words, people of color have learned to notice the subtlest signals and warning signs of bias for one deceptively simple reason: because for us, accurately detecting racial bias is a requirement for survival.

It's exhausting work, and this is why experiencing subtle bias can be *more* harmful to mental health, physical well-being, and executive functioning than experiencing overt bias.[6] In the interest of our safety and our futures, we spend precious cognitive energy turning over every scenario and possible outcome in our minds. The subtler the expression of bias, the more hypervigilance is required to detect it.

THE TRUTH ABOUT MICROAGGRESSIONS

Coming to terms with the fact that bias appears in many forms—from explicit to subtle—can be unsettling. I see this overwhelm every time I teach about bias, and *particularly* when I teach about microaggressions: behaviors that communicate derogatory or negative messages about, or toward, a marginalized group through ambiguous, fleeting experiences that may *seem* small or inconsequential.[7] Because they are so ambiguous, microaggressions typically fall into the third category of "discomfort/unfamiliarity" that Sommers and Norton found in their research. In my experience, the people who have the most familiarity with people of color are the ones who understand the many nuances of this form of bias.

Precisely *because* microaggressions can be so ambiguous, participants in my bias trainings often ask for a list of specific examples so they can avoid committing them. My answer is unsatisfying: Not only will I not provide a list; no such list exists. If it did, it would require constant updates and a heavy disclaimer that what may be a microaggression to one person may be unobjectionable to someone else (remember: Impact carries more weight than intention). The bewilderment I'm met with when I give this answer is palpable. *"How am I supposed to know what to say, or what not to say, if you can't give me a clear answer?"* In that question I hear anger, exasperation, unease, and fear—and above all, a fixed mindset about bias. But I will never be able to give a comprehensive list— because when it comes to microaggressions, there are worlds of nuance to disentangle.

For one thing, the context underlying any remark or behavior plays a significant role in how that action is interpreted. Offhandedly asking a Latina colleague to translate a document from English to Spanish could be described as a microaggression, as it presumes not only that she speaks Spanish but also that she would be inclined (and even willing) to do this additional work beyond the duties listed in her job description. Now, if that colleague had previously shared that she is fluent in Spanish and would happily translate documents with advance notice of the request, the ask takes on a different, and entirely innocuous, tone.

The relationship between the people involved also plays a role. In close relationships where there's a foundation of trust, mutual understanding, and an established track record of unbiased behavior, a joke about how "Asian people are good at math" may be understood as a tongue-in-cheek comment and not a true revelation about that person's beliefs. (User beware, though: I've provided guidance on numerous workplace discrimination complaints stemming from a speaker misjudging how close or casual they could be with colleagues on sensitive topics like this.)

Finally, identity *does* matter—especially yours. In fact, this is the sole premise behind the hilarious "Jokes Seth Can't Tell" segment on *Late Night with Seth Meyers*. In this recurring bit, Seth (a White man) sets up jokes that *would* be racist or homophobic microaggressions, were it not for the fact that two of his writers, Amber Ruffin (a Black woman) and Jenny Hagel (a lesbian), deliver the punch lines. Seth capably models what some White people need to learn: Some jokes just aren't yours to tell.

Microaggressions are subtle, *and* they are harmful. In the most "benign" scenarios, microaggressions highlight someone's difference and mark them as an outsider. In the most harmful scenarios, microaggressions communicate that their identity isn't one to be celebrated at all, but to be resented, leveraged, and/or ridiculed. This is another reason why I reject the request for a "microaggressions checklist." The goal of understanding microaggressions can't simply be to learn what to say or what *not* to say. That's rote memorization, and it instills neither consideration nor compassion. Instead, the focus needs to be on understanding the negative (if often unspoken) impact that microaggressions have, and on believing people of color when we share our experiences. On the latter point, there's a lot of work to do.

THE COMPLAINER EFFECT

People of color have a lifetime of practice in drawing meaning from patterns of behavior, and there's *usually* data to demonstrate that our experience isn't just in our heads. Take that hiring manager, for example. They probably see their unwavering focus on a so-called high bar for talent as evidence of fairness—after all, they believe that the best talent will *always* rise to the top, regardless of race, gender, or socioeconomic status. It might be jarring to learn, then, that the people and organizations that endorse this meritocratic view of success are actually *more* likely—not less—to reproduce gender and racial biases in pay and promotion.[8]

That same hiring manager might also make the argument that, thanks to affirmative action, people of color are no longer disadvantaged in the hiring process and may even have a leg up. But in reality, ample research highlights the discrimination that people of color face at the earliest stages of the hiring process.[9] For example, one set of studies found that Black and Asian job applicants with clear indicators of their race/ethnicity on their résumés fare much worse than those who scrub their résumés of such indicators (i.e., "whiten" their résumés).[10] Specifically, presumed-Asian applicants are 45 percent less likely, and presumed-Black applicants 60 percent less likely, to get an interview callback compared to candidates with "whitened" résumés. And other evidence suggests that, further on in the hiring process, more-qualified candidates of color are often passed over in favor of less-qualified

White candidates.[11] With these data points in mind, it's no wonder that people of color cut their losses at the subtle signs of bias—and organizations miss out on incredibly qualified talent as a result.

To detect subtle bias the way people of color do, White people need to become similarly attuned to these discreet and nuanced signals and learn to interpret them more accurately. Unfortunately, White people often dismiss Black people's interpretations as unfounded. A poignant quote from a Black female participant in a study on anti-Black racism illustrates what this feels like: "Generally, I get myself into trouble because I deal with it [discrimination] head-on. And generally, I'm considered a troublemaker, or someone who's constantly looking at race, and someone who's looking to argue."[12] She was right. Study after study has highlighted how White people view people of color as "complainers" when they attribute their poor treatment to racism or discrimination—a phenomenon known as the "complainer effect."

The first study to center on this paradigm had White participants read a vignette about a Black student who received a low score on an exam.[13] Half of the participants read that the Black student attributed his low score to the poor quality of his answers, and the other half of the participants read that the Black student attributed his low score to racial discrimination on the part of the graders. Then the researchers asked the participants several questions about their perceptions of the student, including the extent to which they thought he was a complainer (e.g., is he hypersensitive, emotional, argumentative) and how likable he seemed (e.g., is he friendly, honest, respectable). As the name of the phenomenon suggests, the Black student was judged as an unlikable and hypersensitive complainer when he attributed his poor grade to discrimination instead of answer quality.[14]

Further studies revealed that there seemed to be no bounds to the circumstances under which someone could be labeled a "complainer." People of color who attribute unfair negative treatment to racial discrimination—*even* when there's explicit evidence that they were, in fact, discriminated against?[15] Complainers. People of color who decry "positive" stereotypes that lead to discrimination (e.g., "You're Asian, so of course you did well on that math test")?[16] Complainers. People of color who talk about racism on social media?[17] You guessed it—complainers.

Often, the complainer effect can stem from a lack of awareness of the conversations happening outside of the all-White bubble. A *Saturday Night Live* sketch, "Election Night," illustrated this brilliantly with its satirical depiction of a watch party for the 2016 presidential election returns.[18] At the top of the scene, one of the White partygoers declares that she can't wait for "this" to be over. For her, the past year and a half of Trump's presidential run was a bad fever dream; her White peers agree, and they begin trading guesses about just how large a margin Hillary Clinton will capture in her inevitable win. The only Black person at the party isn't so sure, but the others miss his skeptical glances and objections to their assertions that Hillary's win is assured. Hours into the party, another Black guest arrives to find that his White friends are shocked and dismayed: It looks like the candidate who spewed hateful rhetoric throughout the campaign could actually win. By midnight, when Alaska is called for Trump, one of the White guests realizes aloud that "America might actually be racist." The Black partygoers feign shock as well—though, of course, they knew America was racist all along (they've never been afforded the luxury of ignorance to that fact). Finally, the White people in the room declare that "this is the most shameful thing America has ever done," at which the Black partygoers erupt in laughter as the scene fades.

As I watched the sketch, I laughed heartily as well. It felt like someone got it. In under six minutes, *SNL* captured why Black people felt so insulted at hearing White people declare, "This is not the America I know," after Trump's election. For communities of color that had faced centuries of oppression in this country, the 2016 presidential election results weren't any new revelation. Those who *were* surprised by the results clearly hadn't spent much time in the presence of people of color—and if they had, they hadn't been listening to them. And there had been plenty of opportunities to do so.

In 2014, one such opportunity caught my attention. It was a campaign on the social media site Tumblr called "I, Too, Am Harvard" (a nod to the Langston Hughes poem, "I, Too"). I scrolled through photo after photo of Black Harvard students holding dry-erase boards on which they had written brief descriptions of the racism they had experienced on campus.[19] Against my better judgment, I also scrolled through the comments section. Scores of commenters derided the Black students, calling them liars, telling them to stop playing the race card, and insinuating that the privilege of attending an elite school like Harvard (which some commenters noted was only because of affirmative action) disqualified them from experiencing any kind of bias. Here were dozens of Black students—sixty-three, to be specific—voicing the truth of their experiences openly, only to be dismissed as hypersensitive complainers. I thought that *for sure* the students' collective voices would change some hearts and minds. One person may be a complainer, but two? Three? Fifteen? *Sixty-three?* How many voices had to echo the same experiences before they were taken seriously—a clear sign of an insidious problem in need of attention?

This question consumed my thoughts and became the focus of my dissertation.[20] The silver lining? I discovered that engaging with stories like those shared by the Black Harvard students could help White people better perceive and respond to bias. In my research, White participants were less inclined to label a Black person as a complainer after reading several stories of discrimination; those same participants also recognized anti-Black bias as a more widespread issue than did those who read only one account of discrimination. Listening to multiple Black voices encouraged them to believe what they heard and shifted their perspectives for the better.

CAN WHITE PEOPLE DETECT
SUBTLE RACIAL BIAS?

Language evolves, and though we may not hear someone explicitly use the word "complainer" these days, the tendency to dismiss people of color who call out racism remains pervasive. Years ago, the common admonishment was to "stop playing the race card"; later, accusing someone of engaging in "identity politics" was the go-to phrase. More recently, "woke" has been co-opted and weaponized in a similar fashion; "stay woke" was once a call to action to stay aware of racism and its impact, but now opponents use it to describe someone who is *too* critical of systems of oppression. At its core, the message behind these "complainer" labels is that people of color—along with their allies—are overreacting or seeing problems where there are none, constructing false narratives, responding disproportionately to the events at hand, and reacting more intensely than how other (White) people would respond if they were in the same position. This begs the question: If White people *did* experience the same kinds of situations, how *would* they respond?

In looking at both Sommers and Norton's research (which showed White people tend to have a narrower definition of racism than people of color do) and the "complainer" research (which found that White people generally dismiss people of color for attributing their treatment in the world to racial bias), *one* conclusion that could be drawn is that White people simply can't detect racial bias the way people of color do—the lived experiences of the two groups are just too distinct to close the gap. But I had a different hypothesis. As I mulled over my own experiences and reconciled them with the research, it occurred to me: Most of the research that had been done up to that point had considered how White people detected bias *against people of color.* But no one had yet explored the distinct—and very important—question: "How do White people detect bias that's *directed at,* rather than *perpetrated by,* their racial group?" In other words, can White people identify racial bias—even in its most subtle forms— when *they're* on the receiving end of it?

The motivating factors that drive people of color to detect subtle bias are unique to our history and lived experiences. With our safety (not to mention our belonging and our thriving) at stake, it's important to identify early warning signs of bias. In this respect, that people of color would adopt a heightened sensitivity and a lower threshold for bias detection makes sense. But White people's motivation typically lands on the other side of the coin: Their goal is to avoid inadvertently confirming that White people are racist.

Understood through this lens, it's understandable that White people would set a much higher threshold for what qualifies as racial bias—otherwise, the sheer number of behaviors that could demonstrate White bias would be overwhelming. I reasoned that, while we knew White people were less likely to detect racial bias against people of color, we knew very little about how White people experienced *anti-White* bias. After President Obama was elected, some White people claimed America had entered a "post-racial era" where White people were suddenly *just as*—if not *more*—likely to be targets of bias than people of color were.[21] What did *those* people consider to be evidence of anti-White bias? And if we could understand that, might we be able to use those insights to help White people detect racial bias against people of color a bit better?

It was a bit of a twisted inquiry for *this* researcher to follow, and I was more than a little apprehensive about taking on a research program devoted to understanding how White people detect anti-White bias. At the time, I was a junior graduate student with no publications to my name, and I was also one of the few Black people in the field of social psychology.[22] It was uncommon enough to find research that really captured the lived experience of being a Black person in America, which includes (but is not limited to) experiencing racism, and here I was, a rare Black person in the field, writing—of all things—about *White* people's experiences with racial bias. I was worried that my program of research would be misinterpreted as an attempt to validate White people's experiences of "reverse racism," and it wasn't hard to imagine the Fox News headline that would result: "Formerly 'Woke' Social Psychologist Proves White People Are the *Real* Targets of Racism." Yet there was something so compelling about the hypothesis: that understanding how White people articulate their experiences with racial bias could unlock some clues about how to help them detect bias against people of color more perceptively and accurately.

WHITE PEOPLE'S EXPERIENCES WITH RACIAL BIAS

In my first study exploring this question—"How do White people detect bias that's directed at their racial group?"— White participants responded to a prompt asking about "a time when someone treated you with prejudice or discriminated against you because of your race/ethnicity." They were given specific instructions to provide as much detail as possible and to take as long as they needed to fully describe the incident. The beauty of open-ended, qualitative data such as essay responses is that they're incredibly rich sources of information; the downside is that they take considerably more work to process than quantitative data does. Thankfully, I had a small team of research assistants helping me. I trained them on the definitions of subtle and blatant racial bias, provided examples of each kind, and turned them loose on the written narratives, asking them to categorize the incidents in each essay as examples of either overt or subtle bias.[23]

Our findings showed that among the two-thirds of White participants who reported experiencing racial bias, seventeen experienced examples of overt bias (such as being called "White girl" in a derogatory tone, or being told they weren't welcome because of their race) and six experienced examples of subtle bias. The subtle examples were especially revealing: Participants wrote of instances where they were the only White person in the room, felt a sense of exclusion, and observed others either watching them intently or deliberately avoiding them. They recalled feeling "extremely uncomfortable" and "kind of hurt because [these people] didn't even know me and were judging me based on the color of my skin." They used descriptors like "awkward," "singled out," and "exposed." One participant described her experience of attending a Baptist church and being the only White person present: "While some people were very inviting and kind," she wrote, "there were a few who would just stare at me or ignore me when we were supposed to be introducing ourselves to people around us." Another participant recalled receiving a similarly cold reception at a party where they were the only White person: "As soon as we walked in the door everyone turned and gave us weird looks."

The most striking aspect of these recollections was that I had frequently heard these same types of stories almost word for word from people of color. And those experiences had a profound impact on them—so much so, in fact, that they could recount the events and encounters in vivid detail, even years later. And as my White research participants narrated their stories, it was clear they didn't think they had overreacted to the events at hand, or that their experiences were insignificant; rather, they trusted their interpretations of the situations and concluded that they had been victims of racial bias. In short, the White participants in my study were quite able to detect subtle racial bias—at least when they were the targets—and it mattered to them. Subsequent research by Dr. Keon West corroborated this.[24] He discovered (unsurprisingly) that people of color experience subtle racial bias more frequently than White people do—but participants of *both* groups found these experiences equally distressing.

Scholars from all disciplines and "anti-woke" pundits have made entire careers from advancing the idea that people of color are erroneously and inordinately responding to negative racial treatment. The research West and I did uncovered an important insight: People of color aren't "complaining" at all. No one likes being treated as inferior because of their race. People of color simply have far more experience with this kind of treatment than White people do.

WHEN EMPATHY ISN'T ENOUGH

During the politically charged months leading up to the 2016 US election, I was a postdoctoral fellow at Purdue University—a predominantly White public university in the Midwest. I was in a wonderful liminal space that gave me access to the professors who were just ahead of me in my career path, as well as to the undergraduate and graduate students I had just left behind. As I listened to their conversations, I noticed a curious pattern emerging: White conservative students were expressing concern about being treated unfairly by their more liberal professors. They admitted that nothing *explicit* was being done to make them feel this way, but they were aware that they diverged from their professors politically, and that feeling of "standing apart" caused them to worry that they'd be graded more harshly and held to a higher standard than their more liberal classmates. Around the same time, similar concerns were being voiced by conservative social psychologists who were worried about experiencing unfair treatment—not getting grants, having their peer-reviewed article submissions rejected—because of their political views. They pointed to demographic data showing just how few social psychologists identified as conservative and called for more support from the governing organization for social and personality psychologists.[25]

Oddly enough, all of this felt exciting and hopeful to me. The feelings the conservative students and social psychologists were openly describing were ones I'd been having for years as a Black woman—underrepresented not only in the field of social psychology but in the broader society as well. I was optimistic that finally, we would be able to have a real conversation about underrepresentation, inequity, and how to solve for both. In response to a particularly active thread on an online discussion forum, several other Black scholars and I coauthored an open letter to the conservative social psychologists' group in which we (in what was surely a surprising turn of events for them) *agreed with the conservative researchers.* We acknowledged that the experience of being underrepresented can be both injurious and unsettling, triggering doubts and insecurities about one's sense of belonging. We validated their concerns about being treated differently and evaluated more harshly because of their identity. How did we know this to be true? Because the experiences they were describing mirrored what people of color had been experiencing for decades. We called on them to reciprocally acknowledge *our* concerns and invited them to cocreate a coalition dedicated to understanding the experiences of underrepresentation—beginning with acknowledging the long-standing history of exclusion people of color faced, and then understanding the ways in which exclusion and underrepresentation impacted groups— like conservatives—that were newer to this experience.

The response was, frankly, nonexistent. For a few days afterward, we received private messages thanking us for speaking out, but the reconciliation I had hoped for never materialized. In fact, many from that group of conservative psychologists redoubled their efforts to protect diversity of political thought, eventually withdrawing from the larger organization for social and personality psychologists altogether and reorganizing under a new banner.

I had thought that highlighting the parallels to the Black experience of bias would elicit empathy among White conservatives, allowing for a productive dialogue on these topics. But the nonresponse to the open letter indicated that, sadly, empathy on its own wasn't enough to overcome the massive psychological barriers keeping White people from detecting racial bias against people of color. White conservatives seemed adept at identifying "bias" against themselves, but they were unwilling to acknowledge the history of racism faced by people of color—or to accept that our experiences were in any way similar to theirs. I was determined to figure out what would foster the kind of empathy and understanding needed to create meaningful conversations around bias.

The common thread linking my eighth-grade White friends baffled (and disgusted) by my hair-care routine, the White participants in the studies I'd read and conducted, and the response from the conservative social psychologists was a significant awareness gap. Each group was unaware of how deeply their White racial identity shaped the way they perceived and navigated the world. Since Whiteness was the unspoken default in their lives, they assumed their experiences were universal. They didn't consider that people with different racial backgrounds might not share these privileges and therefore might encounter the world in a completely different way. I realized that in order for White people to recognize racial bias more accurately, they first needed to understand that Whiteness isn't just a neutral state—it's an identity that profoundly influences everything, from how they're socialized as children and how they're treated as adults to the opportunities they have access to, their treatment by law enforcement and other institutions, their social mobility, and even how they perceive themselves and their place in society.

CHAPTER 4

"White" *Is* a Racial Identity

"My hometown was just named the best place to live in the United States!" Jennifer excitedly announced.[1] She and I worked in the Office of Undergraduate Admissions at Northwestern University together, and because we often introduced ourselves to prospective students by sharing a few details about ourselves, including our hometown, our major, and our favorite thing about school, I knew quite well that she was from a suburb just outside Minneapolis. While Jennifer had painted a charming picture of her hometown, it was a town I'd never heard of before meeting her, and I couldn't imagine it had garnered enough attention to top any national "best places to live" list. Skeptical, I asked to see the list she was talking about, expecting to be presented with some local Minneapolis-area publication as the source of her town's newest accolade. Instead, Jennifer showed me a story published by a mainstream national news outlet that had, in fact, declared her hometown the best place to live in the United States. The list cited factors like affordability, quality of schools, and "intangibles like community spirit" as criteria for earning the top spot.

I was intrigued, and as I scrolled further down the list, it dawned on me what was happening. Before I could stop the words from coming out of my mouth, I exclaimed, "Oh! This is a list of the best cities for *White people* to live in."

Jennifer's eyes widened and she stared at me, frozen. "N–no, it's not," she stammered. "All of these cities are places where *anyone* would love to live, regardless of their race."

I didn't share Jennifer's perspective. As I looked through the list a second time, not a single one of those "best" places seemed like somewhere I'd want to call home. For one thing, they were all predominantly White towns, and I knew from my own upbringing that racial representation in one's city or town mattered a great deal.[2] Growing up in a predominantly White suburb, and later living in coastal cities largely inhabited by White people, I'd become accustomed to navigating the world as the exception rather than the rule. This meant that the hair-care products I needed were confined to the "ethnic" section, the only aisle in the store with a lockbox to safeguard against theft—*if* the products were available at all. It meant that the TV shows I wanted to watch weren't accessible because the cable company determined that there wasn't enough demand to carry stations that catered primarily to people of color.[3] Even the food tasted different![4] It seemed that every interaction I'd had as a person of color in those mostly White places was designed to remind me that I didn't belong, and I couldn't fathom how such places could *ever* be considered "best places to live."

I knew from previous conversations not only that Jennifer—a tall, blond, White, heterosexual young woman—had grown up in a mostly White community but also that the most diverse place she had ever lived was the campus of the college we both attended.[5] I had no doubt that Jennifer believed her hometown was a lovely place, but I just couldn't let her assertion that it would be equally pleasant for people from all races stand. Instead of arguing, I opened a new web page on the computer I was sitting at and typed: "best places to live in the US for Black people." We clicked on link after link and scrolled through the city names together. As I predicted, Jennifer's city was not cited as a "best place to live" on *any* of the lists we found. Instead, the cities that topped *those* lists—among them Atlanta, Washington, DC, and Houston—were much more racially diverse and provided the kind of economic opportunity and general social environment that would contribute to a higher quality of life for Black people.[6] Those lists captured the point I was trying to make: Nice parks, good schools, and "community spirit" can be considered only after the basic needs of belonging, safety, and economic security are satisfied.

To her credit, Jennifer took my feedback in stride. It prompted a conversation about why her hometown—or *any* town, for that matter—may not be experienced the same way by White people and people of color. In Jennifer's world, grocery stores were a wonderland of abundance and choice where all her favorite items were well stocked. She wasn't familiar with having to go to the meagerly stocked "ethnic" aisle of the store, hoping the ingredients she needed to cook dinner were there, lest she have to drive all the way across town to the specialty market. In Jennifer's world, getting her hair and makeup done for prom was as simple as showing up to *any* salon in town and flashing her "inspo pic." She'd never experienced the horror of exiting the shop with foundation three shades too light because the makeup artist was unfamiliar with her skin color, or of having to do her own hair because, halfway through the appointment, the stylist became bewildered by the thickness and volume of her "difficult" curls. In Jennifer's world, a road trip was a carefree experience punctuated by photo ops in quirky roadside towns. She was never forced to learn the mental math that determined when she should preemptively stop for gas and a bathroom break to ensure both a full tank and an empty bladder as she sped through the places that, as a person of color, it wouldn't be safe to stop. While these examples of the differences between Jennifer's (White) world and mine may seem small, they reveal a level of friction that Jennifer never experienced, because she lived in a world that was created for her, by people like her.

Just as Jennifer asserted that her hometown was a place *anyone* would love living, the curators of the "best cities to live in" lists incorrectly presumed that the cities they selected would be universally experienced as wonderful. Intentionally or not, they were basing their decisions on a White default.

THE WHITE DEFAULT

To understand what I mean by the "White default," let's consider a metaphor. Imagine it's Halloween night, and a group of kids are out trick-or-treating, decked out in their costumes and eagerly going door-to-door to collect candy. In this particular neighborhood, there's a policy in place: Every child is to receive two pieces of candy at each house. But when the group of kids reconvenes at the end of the night to compare their candy hauls, something unexpected happens: They discover that *some* among them received an extra treat. The kids who got only the expected two pieces feel slighted, though technically, they received what they were promised. Meanwhile, the children who received the extra pieces of candy feel uncomfortable—perhaps even a bit defensive. After all, they didn't do anything special to earn those additional treats. So, in an effort to justify the difference and to assuage their guilt, they rationalize the situation, convinced that the extra treats must be the result of something they deserve or have earned. Perhaps they invested more effort into their costumes or made a stronger impression when they knocked on doors. On the other hand, maybe the other children were distant or unapproachable, justifying their failure to receive a "bonus treat." The privilege of that extra treat becomes the elephant in the room, and the children separate into subgroups for the rest of the night—the group that got the special treat hanging out in one corner of the room, and the group that didn't assembling in another.

Often when we talk about racial bias, we focus on the *dis*advantages that people of color face. This is, of course, essential to give voice to. However, the negative treatment that people of color experience is just one way in which racial bias manifests. Bias is also expressed in the unfair *advantages* that White people enjoy.[7]

Our society operates much like my fictional neighborhood on Halloween night. Although the explicitly stated rules of engagement claim fairness and equal treatment (*all children* get two treats), the neighborhood's unspoken norms and practices allow White people to benefit from additional privileges (all children get *at least* two treats—but *certain* children receive more than two).

Being White grants privileges and power because society's rules are inherently structured around a White default. This default elevates White people, White culture, and Whiteness itself as the societal norm. It extends beyond grocery store products and hair salon experiences—it's about who is forced to adapt, suppress—or even erase—aspects of their identity to fit in.

For one of the starkest examples of the White default, consider how our characterizations of others never mention race when we're referring to White people, because our audience inherently assumes Whiteness as the default unless we explicitly indicate otherwise. (For instance, while someone might have a "Latina colleague," that coworker is just a "colleague" when she's White.) For most people, the term "Americans" conjures an image of a White person unless we clarify with labels like "African American" or "Asian American."[8] Television shows or movies with all-White casts are categorized by genre (horror, drama, comedy), but shows and movies that do *not* feature White actors are often categorized by their racial focus, garnering awkward and overgeneralized labels like "race-themed" or "Black Stories."[9] "Ethnic" is a modifier used before "food," "clothing," and "neighborhoods" to indicate one thing and one thing only: *not White*. In every case, White characteristics are the benchmark for normalcy, while anything else is a deviation. Our prevailing societal structures and paradigms—from politics to media to economics—are all built to reinforce and perpetuate this default, making it not just the norm but the unquestioned standard.

THE MYTH OF COLOR BLINDNESS

Jennifer's perspective about her hometown, and her presumption of its universal appeal, was likely informed by her adherence to the notion of racial color blindness, or the belief that race *should* not, and *does* not, impact how people are treated, how decisions are made, and how policies are written.[10]

Jennifer didn't come to this conclusion on her own; growing up, members of her (and my) generation would have absorbed the messages (thought to be progressive and anti-racist at the time) imploring people to "not see color." For example, in the nineties, a common school exercise—often incorporated into classroom instruction around Martin Luther King Jr. Day— was to show children one brown egg and one white egg. The instructor would ask students what they noticed about the eggs, and to guess what they might find inside if they cracked both eggs open. Because the eggs were different on the outside, children often presumed that they would be different on the inside as well. But once the eggs were cracked, revealing the same yellowy insides, the lesson emerged alongside the gooey yolks: No matter what we may look like on the outside, we're all the same on the inside. This narrative of color blindness permeated pop culture as well: The all-Black singing group En Vogue admonished listeners to "be colorblind, don't be so shallow" in the chorus of their 1992 hit "Free Your Mind." There was a determined societal push for racial fairness, and it was believed that the best way to get there was to emphasize everyone's sameness.

The problem with color blindness as a racial ideology is that it created a false narrative of the universality of the human experience. At best, it was a misguided attempt at creating equality; at worst, it was deluded magical thinking that inhibited true change. White Americans were so eager to believe that the racial atrocities of the past were finished— or that if racism still existed, it was a problem that *other* people grappled with, not one that was present in themselves or their communities. The inclination to believe this country really was the proverbial "melting pot" where the "American dream" was accessible to anyone who wanted it badly enough and pursued it with enough tireless effort was so strong that they were willing to ignore all evidence to the contrary.[11] The logic went: If we simply pretend everyone is already equal, equality will follow. But what it actually meant was: If we simply pretend everyone is already equal, then nothing needs to change.

Color blindness became a false comfort—a justification for complacency, an exemption from any transformation in actual conduct or attitude. This is perhaps best illustrated by US Supreme Court Chief Justice John Roberts's opinion in *Parents Involved in Community Schools v. Seattle School District*, a case about efforts to diversify a school district. Famously, Roberts declared, "The way to stop discrimination on the basis of race is to stop discriminating on the basis of race."[12] What he offered was essentially the Supreme Court's take on the complainer effect, a reductionist view that sidestepped the core problem: *If you want race to stop mattering, stop talking about how race matters so much.* Ultimately, the pervasive message of color blindness—that we're all the same on the inside and what's on the outside doesn't matter—undermined any attempts to grapple with the vastly different experiences people have precisely because of how they look on the outside.

What we learned from our so-called color-blind approach were two core truths: (1) Color blindness was always a myth (though your "Latina colleague" already knew this), and (2) the only color most White people are *really* blind to is White.

"WHITE" IS A RACIAL CATEGORY WORTH NAMING

Not everyone responds to the revelation of "the White default" as openly as Jennifer did. I've encountered plenty of other White people who bristle at the explicit mention of their Whiteness. In some cases, they insist that they are an individual and do not wish to be categorized by any race at all. In other cases, they become frustrated—and sometimes angered—by the idea that they would even have to name or specify their racial identity (assertions that it's racist to call attention to their race are common in those moments).

These responses underscore the entitlement embedded in the White default: While everyone else is seen as having a race, White people are allowed to simply "be." But the deeper issue with failing to recognize Whiteness as a racial identity is that it obscures the reality that Whiteness shapes White people's lived experience just as profoundly as my Blackness shapes mine.

I once witnessed a textbook example of this during a professional development seminar with a group of law school faculty. The seminar's organizers had specifically asked me to create a workshop that would help the faculty (who were mostly White) have more empathy for the diverse student body that populated their classrooms. Despite hearing from students about how their identities uniquely shaped their engagement with the subject matter, some faculty remained firmly attached to the belief that students should learn to view things "objectively," rather than through the lens of their personal experiences.[13]

It was clear to me that the faculty needed to understand their *own* identities first—a prerequisite for being able to better understand and appreciate the identities of their students—so I crafted an activity that would do just that. First, I asked them to gather in the middle of the room. On the walls surrounding them, I taped pieces of paper, each with a different social identity category (race/ethnicity, gender, religion, sexual orientation, parental status, age, etc.) written on it. I then read prompts, such as *"I think about this aspect of my identity the most,"* and instructed participants to stand beneath the piece of paper that best reflected their response. I love this activity because it usually initiates some profoundly revelatory moments. For example, *"I think about this aspect of my identity the most"* typically evokes a conversation about people's visibly marginalized identities. And another prompt, *"This is the part of my identity that can be most easily concealed [on purpose],"* invites people to examine the reasons they might have for masking certain aspects of their identity, how they feel when they veil parts of who they are, and what the results are (or might be) of revealing those parts when they choose to. But in this group of faculty members, there was one person who seemed committed to shattering my vision for how the activity would unfold.

I read the first prompt. As everyone dispersed to their chosen identity categories, I watched one older White gentleman stand rigid and perfectly still in the center of the room. I did a mental shrug—sometimes participants take a minute to catch on—and proceeded to read four more consecutive prompts. As participants dispersed and returned, *each time,* the same man remained glued to the center of the room. My bafflement increased with each prompt, but with my "good facilitator" hat on, I waited until the exercise was done and asked the faculty to share their reflections. The White professor who'd remained at the center of the room spoke first: "This exercise isn't relevant to me," he asserted. An uneasy silence settled over the room. A few people rolled their eyes and looked exasperated, reactions that told me they had anticipated exactly this kind of response from this person. I took a deep breath before asking my next question: "Tell me what you mean by 'relevant.'"

He replied that he simply "didn't notice" these things— his race, his gender, his first language, or his citizenship—and so he wasn't willing to pretend that he did by walking over to a piece of paper and standing beneath it. I wish I could say I had a well-rehearsed facilitator response prepared for this comment, but in the moment, I was mostly just annoyed. I wanted to roll my eyes, too. Because *of course* he noticed those things—we all do! Within seconds of seeing a person, our brain automatically makes a guess about their race, gender, and age.[14] But my frustration wasn't just about the absurdity of his assertion. It was that he had missed the entire point of the exercise. Had he looked around and reflected on what his peers were doing during the exercise, he would have noticed that in response to the question about which identity people thought of the most, almost all the people of color stood under the "Race/Ethnicity" sign. White people, in contrast, dispersed to other signs aligned with *their* marginalized identities, of which race was not one: Many of the White women stood under the "Gender" sign, and a handful of people went to signs for identities like sexual orientation and age. In other words, each participant stood under the sign representing the social identity category for which they felt they experienced the greatest societal barriers.

Thankfully, another participant—a person of color—soon chimed in, sharing that in their professional environment of mostly White people, they often felt misunderstood and othered. They specifically noted that the people of color who were most successful in this environment were the ones who adopted a White default for how to dress, how to speak, how to teach, and even how to engage in social settings. They explained that they constantly thought about their race precisely *because* they felt unable to fully be themselves; instead, they felt they had to contort and cover in order to fit in.

The stark contrast was readily apparent: The White man didn't think about his race (and therefore found this exercise "irrelevant") because he navigates a world in which his race (and gender, and sexuality, and citizenship status) is the default—allowing him to exist without having to consciously consider or navigate those aspects of his identity. *This* is why the White male professor found it difficult to engage in the identity activity: His Whiteness remained unnoticed and unexamined because it was the societal norm. While his colleagues bemoaned cultural nuances that made it challenging to work, teach, and socialize in ways that felt authentic to them, *he* had the privilege of moving through those spaces without any such challenge. It felt incredibly unfair that he got to be so carefree and dismissive about something that weighed so heavily on so many others.

THE PSYCHOLOGY OF THE WHITE DEFAULT

In my consulting days, I spent a *lot* of time on airplanes. It was common for me to visit three different cities within the course of a week, and a particular point of pride for me was reaching the highest status on American Airlines in a matter of months. My routine was so perfected that I had my timing down to a science: I knew exactly how much time I needed to arrive at the airport, purchase a bottle of Smartwater and a magazine (my "airport indulgences"), and arrive at my gate just as boarding was commencing. Once on the plane, I'd make a beeline to my seat, don my headphones, and tune out from the moment the plane took off until it touched the ground again. I assumed that my air travel experience was one almost everyone else shared, until I came across an article titled "Flying While Fat."[15] In the article, the author described an experience that was markedly different from my own, beginning with the meticulous research required to decide which airline to fly based on the airlines' policies for "customers of size." The author would purchase an extra seat to ensure they had adequate space next to them (though sometimes the flight would be oversold, meaning they'd end up uncomfortably seated next to someone regardless). At the gate, they experienced a deep anxiety in the moments leading up to boarding, anticipating the discomfort and judgment that often accompanied the experience. Once on the plane, as they walked down the aisle, they could feel everyone's eyes on them, silently hoping that they wouldn't take the seat beside them. *Then* they faced the additional agony of having to request a seat-belt extender from the flight attendant. The entire flight experience was one in which they attempted to make themselves as small as possible so as not to disturb their fellow passengers. That meant not going to the bathroom, no matter how uncomfortable they became. It meant staying as still as possible, careful not to encroach on the space of the person next to them. It was an utterly distressing ordeal.

Before reading that article, I rarely, if ever, thought of my body size. I suspect that if I had been asked during a workshop activity how the size of my body impacted me, I would've bristled at the question. I certainly wouldn't have stood beneath a sign that said "Body Size" at any point during the exercise, and perhaps I might even have responded that I didn't have a "body size"—not because I don't have one (if you have body, you undoubtedly have a size), but because I never had to think about mine. But after reading the detailed account of the extra time, financial cost, and psychological effort fat people must spend just to be able to do something I did three times a week without drawing any disquieted stares from strangers, my awareness gap became painfully obvious. My body type is the default, and I benefit considerably from being able to exist in this world *without* having to seek accommodations. I have thin-body privilege.

Looking back on my interaction with the White law professor after reading that article, I could suddenly have more empathy for his position. I'd been asking him to acknowledge his privilege—to consider that there are forces outside of his control that influence how he is treated, supported, and assisted in the world. In a culture that values individualism and rugged self-reliance, the idea of being defined by a collective experience (White, male, heterosexual) felt utterly foreign to him. And so, as far as he was concerned, *I* was refusing to play by the rules—not him—and he lashed out at me, refusing to participate in the activity as a form of protest.

There are lots of examples of White people lashing out against attempts to raise awareness of, and address, racial inequity. Sometimes these are individual moments of protest—like the digital creator who was so incensed by Disney's casting of Halle Bailey (a Black woman) as Ariel in the live-action remake of *The Little Mermaid* that they recolored the entire trailer, frame by frame, to feature a White woman.

Other times, the backlash is much more orchestrated—such as legislation that prohibits schools from teaching about race and racism in both America's history and its present reality.[16] In our research, my colleagues and I uncovered a very predictable set of circumstances that would lead White people to lash out against inclusion efforts: a preference for the status quo, reactance to losing independence, and a belief that equality between groups has already been reached.[17] Each of these carries the same message: *"Our society was getting along just fine before you came in and started sowing seeds of discord with your talk about race and racism."*

But we weren't doing just fine—and we still aren't. However, it turns out that your racial identity plays a significant role in whether you agree with that statement. In one of my favorite studies, when researchers asked participants of *all* races how much progress the United States had made toward equality for racial minorities since the 1960s, they found that White participants, on average, believed there had been more progress made than participants of color did.[18] And a 2011 study revealed that, while both Black and White participants agreed that anti-Black bias had decreased over the decades between the 1950s and the 2000s, White participants believed the decline was much steeper than their Black counterparts did.[19] Moreover, White participants felt that anti-*White* bias had increased significantly in the 2000s—so much so that it surpassed anti-Black bias. In contrast, Black participants saw little change, consistently rating anti-White bias between 1 and 2 out of 10 across all six decades.

One reason for these discrepancies is that White participants are more likely to anchor their comparison of the present to the past, whereas people of color are more likely to anchor their comparison of the present to an ideal future. I see this all the time in my line of work. For example, I sometimes encounter White leaders who are perplexed by their employees' refusal to celebrate the increase in leaders of color from 10 percent to 20 percent. What they fail to see is that their employees of color are looking at those same statistics and wondering why *only* 20 percent of the leaders are people of color. In a comparison between what used to be and where we are now, of course we've made progress. But in a comparison between what is now and what still could be? There is absolutely no contest. We've still got a long way to go.

Unfortunately, there are those White people who don't share this vision for racial progress, because a change to the status quo would require giving up power and control. And it's easy to justify this preference for the status quo if—in comparison to the relatively worse past—the present seems "good enough" that inclusion efforts are no longer necessary. This belief not only allows White people to ignore all manner of current racial ills. It also justifies any backlash against efforts to make Disney movies more racially diverse, educate our children about racism, and improve outcomes for people of color.

At first glance, the backlash against a Black Ariel might seem insignificant. But beneath the surface, it's about preserving a White default that provides a sense of security and continuity—reinforcing the expectation that things will remain as they always have been. As far as many White people are concerned, the titular Little Mermaid has always been White, and therefore she should continue to be White. (Never mind the fact that she's a fictional character, and that her Whiteness is mostly a product of the person who wrote her story.[20]) In the most extreme interpretation, reimagining Ariel as a Black character evidences a slippery slope in which White people could be completely erased.

The resistance to anti-racism education is an even starker example of how the concern for maintaining the status quo is *really* just about power and control. The most prominent headlines about the national backlash against teaching about racial inequity have rightfully focused on the impacts to school curricula, library bookshelves, and the next generation's understanding of the world. Fewer have focused on another interesting detail: Laws like Florida's 2022 Stop WOKE Act give parents the power to file objections to any material they find offensive. For White parents who feel powerless in a system that's "indoctrinating" their children, the law is as much about limiting what's being discussed in schools as it is about regaining a lost sense of control and dominance in an ever-changing world.

When grown adults are arguing over whether a fictional character "can be" Black, and others are attempting to rewrite history to highlight the so-called useful skills enslaved people acquired, it feels laughable to suggest that *this* is what racial nirvana looks like.[21] And yet, memorable milestones toward racial equality can sometimes obscure the work left to do. After Barack Obama was elected president in 2008, many proclaimed we had reached a "post-racial era." They reasoned that if America could elect a Black man president, surely the country had evolved beyond its racial struggles, leaving those injustices in the past. Some wondered if this was what the "new America" would look like, and they provided data to support their projections: By the year 2050, White people would be outnumbered by people of color and would become the new racial minority. While some celebrated these manifestations and projections of racial progress, they had the opposite effect on many White people, who saw them as a threat.[22]

Perhaps this is why the years following Obama's presidency saw a sharp rise in racial backlash, culminating in the election of Donald Trump in 2016. His campaign, fueled by nativist rhetoric and promises to "take back" America from immigrants, resonated with many White voters who felt uneasy about the country's demographic shifts. Research shows that racial resentment was a strong predictor of Trump support, with studies indicating that White Americans who thought of increasing racial diversity as a threat were significantly more likely to vote for him.[23] This backlash extended beyond politics, manifesting in anti-DEI policies, book bans, and laws restricting discussions of race and racism in schools—all efforts to reinforce the status quo and push back against the changing racial landscape.

ESTABLISHING A NEW DEFAULT

Earlier, I told the story about how reading the "Flying While Fat" article opened my eyes to the ways I have benefited from the thin-person default that exists in our society. While I'm grateful that I came across that article, I'm also a little embarrassed to admit that it was a *magazine* that made me aware of my body-size privilege, and not a firsthand encounter with a fat friend or colleague. Looking back on that period of my life, I realize now that I could have easily traded outfits with most of my closest friends during those years. I likely wasn't aware of my privilege in part because my friends were not remotely diverse in body size.

For White people, the same is often true when it comes to the racial makeup of their friend groups. The Public Religion Research Institute, a think tank that explores religious attitudes in America, found that, in 2013, White Americans' friendship groups were 91 percent White, and that three-fourths of White Americans (75 percent of survey respondents) had friendship groups that were *entirely* White.[24] Nearly ten years later, the results of that survey were largely the same: White Americans' friend groups were 90 percent White, and most White people *still* had entirely White friendship groups—though this time the figure was 67 percent of respondents, marking a small improvement from the 2013 data.[25] Just as my mostly skinny friends kept me oblivious to my thin privilege, these homogeneous friendship networks preclude an awareness of racial privilege. For White people with White friends, racial identity is barely noticeable (until they're confronted with it outside of their social circles), because everyone's racial identity is the same. This makes it easy to take for granted, on a day-to-day basis, that there's a world of other identities and experiences out there.

The antidote to this complacency is to learn to exist in spaces where Whiteness is not the racial default. This is about more than having a racially diverse friendship group; it's about seeking out experiences that teach you what it's like to move through the world without the tailwind of being the presumed default. You'll never understand what it's like to be a person of color in a White-dominant society, but you *can* intentionally put yourself in environments where you're not in the majority to gain a small glimpse of what it means to navigate the world as a minority.

For many people, traveling to a different region or country can provide this perspective. Years ago, when I got lost on the metro in Tokyo, I was so grateful that the clerk at the subway station patiently communicated with me through Google Translate to help me find my way (instead of yelling, "This is Japan! Learn to speak Japanese!" as many Americans do at people speaking languages other than English in this country).

Travel isn't the only way to generate those empathy-building experiences. I'm an avid fiction reader, and years ago I realized my personal library was filled with books about White people, written by White people. I was eager for more representation of my own culture in the books I consumed, and I also saw an opportunity to explore people, places, and cultures that are different from mine. My first attempts at this were a little taxing. When I first picked up Chitra Banerjee Divakaruni's *Sister of My Heart,* my brain plodded, molasses-like, through the text as I struggled to pronounce and remember the characters' names. I realized that my brain had grown accustomed to American and/or Anglicized names, and I had to push past my inclination to skip over what felt unfamiliar and "unpronounceable." Over time it got easier, but only because I consciously chose to retrain my mind to embrace a more inclusive default— one that welcomed a variety of names, settings, and stories featuring a diverse range of characters, rather than defaulting to the White narratives I had come to know.[26]

Our increasingly diverse workplaces provide additional opportunities to expand our perspectives. As a Christian, and as an American, it may feel natural to me to ask someone about how they plan to spend Christmas or the Fourth of July, but in a diverse workplace, we might come into contact with a whole host of religious and cultural observances beyond those that center Christianity or the United States. For example, I used to know nothing about Lunar New Year (and believed it was only called "Chinese New Year" until a Vietnamese colleague pointed out that *many* Asian nations— not just China—celebrate that time of year). Then, the first time I tried out the "Happy New Year!" greeting, I received a gentle correction to include a blessing or well-wish instead of just saying "Happy New Year." By embracing situations where I *wasn't* the default—either in the language I spoke, the identity centered in my imagination, or the cultural observance I was recognizing—I was able to expand my perspective.

There may be many reasons why you don't hear firsthand experiences of what it's like to be a person of color. Perhaps your friendship network *is* entirely White. If that's the case, do everything you can to seek out, and listen to, people of color. If you *do* have people of color in your life, ask yourself whether their thoughts and perspectives are considered central to the conversation. If they're not, it's time to really listen. The next time one of them makes a side comment that gets overlooked by the group, bring attention back to it. Even better, actively seek out their opinions and experiences: How do they feel about a particular social issue? What resonated for them in the movie you just saw together, or in the book they just finished reading? What's their perspective on the headline news today? How did it feel for them to be at that gathering you were all at this weekend? Take a page from the research showing that in interracial interactions, people with a growth mindset view feedback from the person they're engaging with as equally important as—if not more important than—their own perspectives and experiences in the encounter.[27] The point is to meaningfully include them as active participants in the conversation.

Another way to gain perspective on the benefits (i.e., privilege) that the White default affords is to read about experiences unlike your own. Find a racial equivalent of the "Flying

While Fat" article and really engage with the content. You may use the notes at the end of this book as a starting point, but seeking out content based on your unique preferences will help ensure that your pursuit of diverse voices has staying power. If you, like me, love fiction, challenge yourself to read stories featuring characters from a wide range of cultures and with a rich multitude of experiences. (If you like tales about quirky families, *The Wangs vs. the World* by Jade Chang will delight, and I will *always* recommend *Homegoing* by Yaa Gyasi—a story about the impact of slavery that spans generations.) If you prefer nonfiction, check out books or articles that provide unique perspectives on history and/or current events. (Perhaps Carol Anderson's *White Rage* or Roxane Gay's *Bad Feminist* will pique your interest!)

But reading isn't enough, so don't stop there. One of my favorite ways to use social media is to gain perspectives from people who represent all different communities and experiences. I often start by following those authors or leaders whose ideas resonate with me, and let the algorithms take things from there.[28] You can also make this a group activity! I once kicked off a team meeting with an icebreaker in which I asked everyone to share the Instagram accounts they were following that challenged them or made them think differently. The discussion that followed was thrillingly generative. Once you start following those accounts, listen to and consider the ideas shared therein. When you hear something that challenges you and quickens your pulse, take that as a sign to dig in. Then get off social media and connect in real life. Attend a community event that brings together panelists to discuss a topic with the kind of nuance that a thirty-second video precludes. Tell a friend about something you learned and ask them for their perspective. Use the forces of the internet to help curate a *more* diverse understanding of the world, rather than another echo chamber.

When you have these conversations, explicitly talk about all racial identities—including White ones. For those of us raised in a society that prizes color blindness, this can be an unsettling new practice. However, when we begin to realize that who we are shapes the way we experience the world, we begin to understand what those faculty members in my workshop learned: that other people will necessarily experience the world differently because of their unique combinations of identities. Instead of focusing only on what makes us the same, we can celebrate those similarities *and* value the differences that shape each person's perspective.[29] It might sound counterintuitive, but fully acknowledging Whiteness as a racial identity—and all the benefits and privileges that go along with it—will make you more equipped to detect bias.

CHAPTER 5

The Magnitude of White Privilege

As a young Black woman who wanted to one day have children, I'd always been marginally aware of all the evidence that my becoming pregnant and having a baby in the United States could quite literally be deadly. For one, there were the appalling statistics: Black women in the United States are three times more likely to die from pregnancy-related causes than White women are.[1] For another, there were the narrative accounts of childbirths that ended in tragedy, like when a well-known hospital in my area left a Black family grieving after a woman died following a planned cesarean section.[2] Doctors had performed a procedure that typically takes forty-five minutes in just seventeen, didn't properly suture the mother, and refused to readmit her despite signs she was bleeding internally. I'd heard the stories and was acquainted with the data. But even with that knowledge, I was young and naïve, convinced these were statistics that applied to, and fates that befell, "other people." Surely, they weren't relevant to me.

But as my husband and I became more serious about trying to conceive, I gathered increasing evidence that a life-threatening pregnancy or delivery wasn't an abstract phenomenon that happened to "other people" but a real possibility for me. The more I consulted friends and friends of friends about their birthing experiences, the more I discovered that for every Black friend of mine who'd had a beautiful childbirth experience, there was another who could barely talk about her traumatic birth story at all. These women told harrowing stories of close calls because doctors dismissed their concerns or complaints, or scary postdelivery experiences that happened with seemingly no explanation, like one first-time mom who was paralyzed from the waist down for weeks after her delivery. They spoke of the authoritative and condescending tones their doctors took, and how intimidating it could be to ask questions or push back against proposed approaches. I could hear the urgency in their voices as they shared with me the information they wished they'd known sooner.

I was given a list of questions to ask when interviewing healthcare providers, and the woman who shared it implored me to find a caregiver I could trust to look out for me in those high-stress, high-risk birthing moments. She elaborated that having my (Black) husband in the room would not be enough, and that my birth team should include a doula—a trained professional who would advocate on my behalf and guide me through the delivery process.[3] Ever the diligent student, I took copious notes, saved their spreadsheets and documents in a folder on my computer, and prepared for the road ahead. Armed with a wealth of information, I felt confident that I would be able to handle whatever came my way.

Then, in April 2022, Serena Williams published an essay detailing her near-fatal experience with a blood clot after delivering her daughter Olympia.[4] She described waking up paralyzed, with coughs that wracked her body and risked popping her stitches, and the foggy but grim realization that she was dying. She recounted pushing through the physical and mental haze to advocate for herself, drawing upon her personal medical history when appealing to a nurse, only to be dismissed: "I think all this medicine is making you talk crazy." Serena Williams was hardly the first Black woman to have this experience, but her essay was sobering. Her prowess on the tennis court has earned her the title of GOAT (greatest of all time), along with the social standing, accolades, and financial resources that most of us can only dream of—not to mention a heightened awareness of her body thanks to her career as a professional athlete. Yet none of those advantages safeguarded her. The resulting question was terrifying: If *Serena Williams* couldn't get her medical team to take her seriously, what hope did the rest of us have?

Serena's influence captured national attention and ignited a conversation—not only about the issue of Black maternal mortality rates but also about potential solutions. I was optimistic that change was on the horizon. No longer would Black women have to rely on a patchwork of information gathered from private conversations with our friends and friends of friends to protect us; the system was going to take us, our needs, and our *lives* seriously. But systemic reform takes time, and I was suddenly on a deadline: In May 2022, I learned that I was pregnant with our daughter, Georgia. And so, elated about the imminent addition to our family while also soberly aware of what could be on the horizon, I took my computer folder full of information, adopted an unapologetic nature à la Serena Williams, and set about building my birth team.

My discussions with prospective OBs and midwives followed a consistent pattern: They all thoroughly addressed my inquiries about the pregnancy experience, assured me they'd be readily accessible throughout the process, and the like. But beyond these considerations (which were important!), I was really looking for a deeper sense of connection and trust—that "special something" that indicated this person was committed to prioritizing my safety and my well-being, whatever unfolded in the delivery room. After a few interviews, it seemed I had found that person. The doctor was a White woman around my age who shared my love of nail art and exhibited an incredible bedside manner. From the moment she walked into the exam room, I felt as though she had infinite time and undivided attention for me. She pulled a chair close to me and leaned in as I shared my journey up to that point with her.

The conversation felt easeful and intimate—almost familial. And yet, I had some reservations about having a White woman as my doctor. Would she be able to truly understand, let alone take seriously, the unique concerns I had as a Black woman? I took a deep breath and addressed the issue head-on: "Another question on my mind is about my safety. I'm sure you've seen the essay Serena Williams wrote about her post-birth experience, and I know the Black maternal mortality rate in the US is quite high. I'm so thrilled to be pregnant, but I'm also terrified of losing my life while doing this." After a moment's pause, my prospective doctor said, "I'm glad you asked this question. It's a very important topic." She continued earnestly. "And I want you to know that there's no systemic racism at our practice." She went on to detail the variety of implicit bias trainings each doctor had undergone, along with the channels available for submitting feedback or complaints if I ever felt I experienced discrimination.

As the doctor spoke, two truths became clear to me. For one, the composure with which she responded clarified that *this* was my doctor. When I broached the topic of race and shared my fears as a Black woman, she remained open— showing no tension, discomfort, or defensiveness at the suggestion that the staff, the system, or even she herself might hold racial biases. Instead, her response indicated that she saw my question as an invitation to dialogue rather than a veiled accusation. Her body language suggested that she had considered and/or discussed this matter before, which gave me the nonverbal affirmation and encouragement I was looking for. I had no concerns that she was personally harboring anti-Black bias that would emerge down the line.

But the second thing that became clear was this: My doctor had little idea what systemic racism was.

THE PUZZLE OF THE EXTRA PRIZE

It's true that acknowledging one's Whiteness is a significant step on the journey to identifying racial bias. Yet treating identity and privilege as purely personal—rather than things that are systemically conferred—oversimplifies the issue. To illustrate, let's return to the Halloween analogy from chapter 4. Recall that the policy dictating that all trick-or-treaters receive two pieces of candy failed to prevent an unfair outcome. Upon closer examination, it also resulted in some lingering questions—including who was responsible for the fact that some kids ended up with more candy than others. How we answer that question about responsibility depends on whether we view the issue through an *interpersonal* lens or a *systemic* one.

An interpersonal approach to explaining this disparity would place responsibility on individual neighbors who chose to give extra treats to *some* children but not to others. For example, we may question whether the adults handing out the extra candy were conscious of their actions. Maybe they'd been informed of the rule (everyone gets two pieces of candy) but didn't follow it—either because they willfully ignored it (explicit bias) or because they unintentionally ignored it (implicit bias). Over time, the narrative might evolve to imply that there's something wrong with the children who didn't get the extra prize: Maybe their treatment was warranted because they were disrespectful or their costumes were threadbare and unimaginative. Whatever explanation we settle on, an interpersonal focus leads us to conclude that the *discrete individuals* involved in the trick-or-treating were responsible for the day's disparate outcomes.

In the real world of racial inequity, these same kinds of explanations abound. The police officer who tickets a Black man for speeding but lets a White woman off with a warning isn't aware of his lopsided application of the rules; to address this, he's assigned a training session to get a refresher on precinct policy. The supervisor who gives critical performance feedback to an employee of color who makes mistakes on a client memo but grants leeway to a White employee who commits the same errors is removed from managerial responsibilities to solve the problem. The interpersonal approach is often applied to people of color as well (the analogous trick-or-treaters who missed out on the extra prize). For example, when presented with data showing disparities in promotion between employees of color and White employees, leaders determine that the gap must be because of a skill deficit among the former group—so they develop professional development programs to help people of color "build those necessary skills." Individual bias certainly plays a significant role in these examples, but individual bias alone can't explain the persistent patterns that emerge from countless decisions made by many people over time.

Systemic racism is what happens when these small advantages accumulate. That police officer is not a lone actor; indeed, evidence suggests that people of color are not only more likely than White people to get speeding tickets; they're also more likely than White people to get pulled over in the first place.[5] And that supervisor who evaluates White employees more leniently than employees of color isn't alone either; lots of people make that exact same judgment call.[6] Moreover, that company's racial promotion disparities are not due to a "skill deficit"; people of color are often *more* qualified for positions than their White counterparts but are nevertheless overlooked for a whole host of reasons.[7] Disparate treatment is built into the rules and norms—both written and unwritten—that govern the decisions and behaviors of an entire society. This results in a collective mindset that, over time, yields a fundamentally different life experience for one group than for another.[8]

When viewed through this systemic lens, we see that the reason White people are more successful than people of color is because the rules that govern our society are designed to support and prioritize White experiences—created by them, with their perspectives and needs at the center. This has been the case for centuries: The White people who colonized the United States brought with them beliefs about their inherent superiority. These beliefs were advantageous, as they allowed the settlers to justify their treatment of both the Indigenous people who lived here and the slave labor they used to develop the land. Then they codified those beliefs into laws that would preserve their power and superiority for generations to come.

So what does all of this have to do with my doctor?

PEELING BACK THE LAYERS OF SYSTEMIC RACISM

When my doctor answered my question by referencing the bias trainings that individuals in her practice had completed, she was conflating *interpersonal* expressions of bias with *systemic* expressions of bias. Of course, some doctors surely carry unexamined biases. But what my doctor failed to account for is the fact that even if there were no such doctors in that particular hospital, *the system itself* is already set up to preclude people of color from enjoying the same positive (read: non-life-threatening) experiences that White patients do. In other words, no matter *how* unbiased individual practitioners are, they're still practicing within a system that perpetuates racial inequities. Racism is as much about preestablished rules and preexisting regulations as it is about the beliefs or actions of the humans who uphold and enforce them.

For example, systemic racism in healthcare manifests long before a patient enters the doctor's office. There's bias baked into the very process that determines whether a patient has insurance, what kind of insurance they have, and what procedures are covered by that insurance. In the United States, at least, a person's employment status and job type factor significantly into the kinds of health insurance available to them. This means that people in higher-wage, salaried jobs (which are predominantly held by White people) have greater access to quality health insurance than people in lower-wage, hourly jobs (which are predominantly held by people of color).[9] Which insurance you have (high-quality or low-quality) dictates your ability to schedule an appointment with a specialist directly, rather than wait weeks for a referral that may never come. It can also be the difference between paying thousands of dollars out of pocket for a procedure deemed "unnecessary" by your insurer, and paying a twenty-dollar copay because your top-notch healthcare plan covers that procedure.

We can trace the roots of this systemic bias even deeper when we ask ourselves *how* insurance providers decide which treatments to cover. These determinations are based, at least in part, on medical research on different ailments. But therein lies another problem: Medical research continues to be heavily based on studies involving men and White participants.[10] For example, one study found that *99 percent* of the studies on aging erroneously conclude that male and female patients will experience similar outcomes, because they overlook the meaningful impact of menopause on female aging.[11] This oversight is largely due to the fact that those 99 percent of studies on aging were conducted primarily on men, leading to significant gaps in understanding women's health. Moreover, a recent investigation found that just 5 percent of participants in clinical trials in the United States are Black patients.[12] This lack of comprehensive research into the unique experiences of people from different demographics can lead to all manner of faulty—and fatal—conclusions. For example, until 2021, the algorithm that doctors used to assess kidney function consistently underestimated the severity of kidney disease in Black patients because the formula relied on an outdated (and completely inaccurate) belief about differences in creatinine levels between White and Black people. After the equation was finally corrected, more than *fourteen thousand* Black patients had their positions on the transplant list moved up, decreasing their wait times by an average of *two years*. For as long as White people (and White men in particular) remain the predominant subjects of clinical research and trials, medical data will continue to suggest that the most important ailments for doctors to focus on—and the most important ailments for insurance companies to cover—are those that overwhelmingly impact White people (and White men in particular).[13] Other demographics will necessarily be left behind.

As one final example of the systemic issues embedded in the US healthcare system, consider who is responsible for training our medical professionals: 2018 data from the Association of American Medical Colleges indicates that approximately 64 percent of US medical school faculty are White.[14] Why does this matter? Because a White doctor (and/or a doctor who has worked mostly with White patients) is more likely to underestimate—or to inaccurately characterize altogether—the prevalence and severity of medical issues that predominantly impact people from different racial and ethnic backgrounds.[15] And without a personal connection to those systemic biases, White medical school faculty may see the racial disparities in outcomes as mere statistics on a page—not an urgent public health crisis—and may unintentionally perpetuate these disparities, whether by omitting them from their curricula or by evading classroom discussions on the subject.

The reality is that all of these examples of systemic racism could be upheld and perpetuated by people who may not harbor any individual racial biases themselves. Whether or not my doctor took implicit bias training would have no bearing on whether the medical books she consulted contained information about the comorbidities of uterine fibroids—a condition with an especially high incidence among Black women. Whether or not my doctor's office had a discrimination complaint portal wouldn't impact my insurance company's determination that my blood tests during early pregnancy would be out of policy. In fact, my doctor might disagree with those decisions and do everything she could to challenge them—but none of that would change the rules.

THE COMPOUNDING IMPACT OF
SYSTEMIC RACISM

Years ago, I worked as a consultant for a production company's nascent DEI committee. The committee—composed of two Black women, three White women, and two White men—was proportionally much more racially diverse than the company it represented, which I took to be a good sign. Another good sign was that there was leadership buy-in for this work: One of the White men on the committee, Peter, was the company's cofounder.[16] During our first group meeting, everyone was courteous and good-humored, but tensions arose as we began to address the work ahead of us. One such conflict emerged when Peter expressed discontent with his Black female colleague's description of the company as racist during a previous conversation. He argued that for someone to be racist, they had to have racism "in their heart," and he drew on the Merriam-Webster definition of racism to prove his point: "a belief that race is the primary determinant of human traits and capacities and that racial differences produce an inherent superiority of a particular race."[17] While he conceded that there *was* work to do to bring more people of color into the company, Peter emphasized that none of the leaders at his company believed in the inherent superiority of White people. It stood to reason, then, that the company was not racist.

Peter's reaction revealed a gap in how he thought about racism. Like my doctor, he failed to see that racism extends beyond individual actions and operates on a much broader systemic level. He didn't consider that, because his company was predominantly White, and because getting ahead in the entertainment industry depends largely upon one's connections, and because White people generally have White networks, even if the White people at his company didn't harbor beliefs about the superiority of White people, they would still reinforce both societal and industry inequities in their organization simply because they were operating the way they always had. He couldn't see what his Black colleague knew to be true: The company was a microcosm of the racist society in which it was operating. And if the company allowed *those* inequities to persist unchecked, then the company was racist, too.

During our time together, I worked with Peter to help him understand his Black colleague's perspective. It began with inviting him to change his level of focus. Rather than emphasizing the hearts, minds, and behaviors of individuals, Peter needed to realize that systemic inequality could only be identified by paying attention to the broader patterns that played out across entire groups of people within a society.

Over the course of my career, I've worked to find a clear way to help folks like Peter see the cumulative impact of all the "small" advantages White people experience over time. One of my favorite illustrations comes from a workshop on bias that I used to co-facilitate with my friend and business partner, Jon Feingold. In our sessions, Jon, a White man, and I, a Black woman, frequently drew upon our own identities to illustrate the way systemic racism reinforces and perpetuates itself to produce dramatically different outcomes for people from different racial groups. In this particular workshop, we introduced a hypothetical in which Jon and I worked at a company that utilized monthly performance reviews to dictate whether an employee would keep their job or be fired. The good news, the hypothetical company leaders assured us, was that to keep things "fair," these determinations would be data driven. To create a set of standards, they conducted an in-depth analysis of previous performance evaluations and built an algorithm that factored in historical results to predict future performance. The algorithm suggested that White men had a 99.5 percent chance of advancing every month, and Black women had a 98.5 percent chance of advancing, so that rule was applied to our individual cases. But while those odds may *look* close enough, that small difference proved significant when compounded over multiple decisions: After an eight-year period of employment, Jon's chances of still being employed were 61.8 percent, while mine were only 23.4 percent. The problem? The company had used historical data to inform its algorithm, and—because past reviews had been shaped by subjective judgments, systemic inequities, and unconscious bias, favoring White men over Black women—the algorithm *reinforced* those patterns rather than *eliminating* them.

This hypothetical was obviously deliberately crafted to make a point. But it's not so far-fetched. Our day-to-day existence is governed by so many rules that either increase or decrease our chances of a favorable outcome. In many cases, every one of these discrete advantages compounds over time, accumulating to create a life with less friction, more ease, expanded opportunities, and better outcomes. Small disparities compound into significant ones; this is both a mathematical and a societal truth.

The compounding effect doesn't just apply to advantages and privileges; *dis*advantages and obstacles multiply as well. Consider a young man of color who lives in a neighborhood under more frequent police surveillance than the adjacent White neighborhood for no other reason than its demographic makeup. Because there's more surveillance in his neighborhood, this young man is more likely to be taken into police custody under mere suspicion of wrongdoing. He misses a day of work as a result, and because he, as a person of color, is less likely to have a job that offers paid time off, his absence means no pay for that day, a strike against him at work, and a reputation as an unreliable employee— meaning he's more likely to be fired down the line (if he's not fired on the spot, that is). Meanwhile, he may never recover the belongings—cash, cell phone, and the like—that were confiscated during his brief time in police custody, exacerbating his financial loss. This interaction with the criminal justice system—being handcuffed, interrogated by police, and treated as a second-class citizen—causes psychological trauma that impacts his sleep, mood, and general functioning. The one "bad day" at the police station results in a stretch of difficult days, weeks, and even months—not because he

committed a crime (he didn't) but because of heightened surveillance in the neighborhood he was born in—a direct result
of long-standing systemic bias.

These are the realities that lie behind headlines about the
"punishing reach" of racism.[18] For instance, one large-scale
study led by researchers at Stanford, Harvard, and the US
Census Bureau found that White boys raised in affluent families would likely remain rich into adulthood, but Black boys
raised in affluent families had only a 17 percent chance of
growing into rich adults—indeed, they were more likely to
experience poverty as adults than they were to maintain their
wealth.[19] With these data in mind, the "racial wealth gap"—
White households had a median net worth of $250,400 in
2021 compared to $48,700 for Hispanic households and
$27,100 for Black households—is wholly unsurprising.[20] Fac-
tor in how criminal convictions directly hurt earning power
(consider our innocent young adult above) and how unequal
access to healthy food and quality healthcare both directly
and indirectly impact wealth (e.g., more out-of-pocket doctor's visits, more unpaid sick days, more prescription drugs)—
to name just a few of the systemic inequalities that exist—and
we see how the racial wealth gap is the inevitable and cumulative outcome of a system built to privilege White people.

The sheer truth—and the sheer scale—of the matter is difficult to absorb. It's overwhelming to learn about, and it's overwhelming to write about. And this sense of overwhelm may

seem like a valid reason to disengage, to say, *"There's nothing I can do to influence a situation of this magnitude,"* and to bury your head back in the comfortable sand.

My doctor, in actively listening to my concerns and engaging me in a discussion to help put my mind at ease, made a different choice. Doing so buoyed our relationship *and* changed the way she practiced medicine for the better. I know this because when I became pregnant again, I looked forward to seeing her. During our first checkup, she shared how much that conversation two years prior had impacted her thinking and changed her behavior. She admitted that she shouldn't have waited for me to broach the question of systemic racism in the maternal healthcare space, and shared that she now proactively raises the topic with her Black patients. (It warmed my heart to know just how much of an effect our discussion had on her, but I also chuckled internally when she opened with "You might not even remember this, but..." If only she knew just how impactful the conversation was for me, too!)

Peter—the cofounder of the production company whose DEI committee I consulted for—also chose not to retreat from the issue. In fact, over the several months that we worked together, I watched Peter's perspective transform in real time. He came to realize that the reason he'd initially taken such offense at the accusation that his company was racist was because he mistakenly believed that his colleague was calling *him* racist. But once Peter began to see himself as distinct from the system he exists in, he came to realize that his colleague's comment wasn't a personal attack—on *any* one person—at all. He saw that the expressions of racism we see today spring from the seeds of ideas that were planted centuries ago—ideas that took deep root in our society and became the foundation of every institution built. And he was ready to do his part to dismantle it. How did Peter get there?

LEARNING TO RECOGNIZE
WHITE PRIVILEGE

When I work with people like Peter, my first step is typically to help them recognize their White identity (as discussed in chapter 4) and acknowledge the ways it has shaped their lives. This is critical, because without an understanding of their racial identity and the ways their Whiteness informs their lived experience, White people will mistakenly assume that everyone gets the benefit of the doubt in life: If it's how the world works for them, then surely it's how the world works, period. It's generally not until they glance into their Black neighbor's trick-or-treat bag and see vastly fewer treats that it occurs to them otherwise. In short, detecting systemic racism begins by learning to detect systemic *racial privilege*. And detecting privilege means accepting that at least *some* treatment can be attributed to our group identity—not to our individual actions or our personal worthiness.

Once, a White person who was very close to me asked what White privilege was, and after I gave an explanation, the person said, "That's interesting. Maybe I'll experience privilege at some point. So far I've had to earn everything I get. Such is life." I was baffled by the response, particularly because some of the defining characteristics of that person's life narrative—dropping out of college, inheriting a successful family business, and ultimately deciding to return to college and pursue a second career in their sixties—would have resulted in very different outcomes had they been a person of color. This person had undoubtedly worked very hard to achieve (and maintain) what they had gotten (and been given). At the same time, their racial privilege undoubtedly played a significant role in ensuring that their hard work paid dividends. What this person couldn't see in that moment was that, had they not been born White, they would've had to work even *harder* to earn, and keep, everything they now had—*if* they ever earned it at all.

Sometimes, privilege manifests as positive experiences that your race benefits from while others do not. Other times, it means that challenges—ones people of *all* races may face—remain difficult, but not life-altering or catastrophic. Acknowledging White privilege doesn't mean you've had an easy life without strain or toil, drudgery or debt or difficulty. Instead, it means acknowledging your access to what Dr. Peggy McIntosh calls the "invisible knapsack" filled with tools and resources to help you *overcome* that difficulty—tools and resources that people of color simply don't have.[21] As Drs. L. Taylor Phillips and Brian S. Lowery eloquently state, "Racial privilege manifests most clearly when it shields

White victims of hardship from the worst possibilities. For instance, joblessness is less likely to lead to homelessness, crimes are less likely to result in jail time, and illness is less likely to result in death for Whites compared to minorities."[22]

Why is it such a big deal if White people overlook the role racial privilege has played in their lives? Because White people who deny the individual impact of White privilege are more likely to think that *everyone* should be able to overcome hardship. This lack of empathy undergirds their failure to understand the ways that race and racism impact others' lives and erodes their support for policies that aim to promote racial justice and equity.[23] The logic then extends in detrimental fashion: *"I had a run-in with the police once, and I walked away unscathed. That means* you, too, *could've walked away unscathed—if only you'd dressed better, been more respectful, or complied with the officer's demands."* In a world where White people *believe* this, systemic intervention for police brutality becomes unnecessary—because they don't see police brutality as a systemic problem.[24]

Recognizing privilege can feel shameful, but it doesn't have to. Although it may be uncomfortable to learn that some unearned advantages have aided you in life (i.e., that "invisible knapsack"), focusing on shame only prompts us into maladaptive coping strategies like denial and defensiveness. In a society that tells us that some identities are more valued than others, privilege is simply a matter of fact. Once you accept White privilege as a reality, you can learn how to wield it to create a more equitable society.

SHARE YOUR CANDY

Systemic racism is upheld by individual decisions that reinforce a collective belief. Systemic racism can be *undone* by individual decisions as well—when recipients of privilege make the conscious choice to promote racial equity by sharing their privilege with others.

In 2018, actresses Jessica Chastain and Octavia Spencer made headlines after Spencer, a Black woman, revealed during a Women Breaking Barriers panel at the Sundance Film Festival that when Chastain had learned that Spencer was woefully underpaid relative to her, Chastain committed to building a clause into her contract requiring that she and Spencer get paid the same amount for their next film together.[25] After a bidding war on a new project, Spencer ended up earning *five times* what her rate would have been without that clause.

That's what can happen when White people truly become aware of their privilege, *without* feeling shame or defensiveness about the unearned advantages they've experienced. They wake up to the fact that not everyone has access to that invisible knapsack filled with resources to help them navigate life, and to the fact that, while their success may be a product of hard work, grit, persistence, and determination, it's also undeniably linked to that knapsack and the advantages it confers upon them. Newly aware of that knapsack, they share the resources within it—like Chastain did when she used her star power to advocate for Spencer. Doing so was a huge risk:

The studios could have passed on the movie, deeming it too expensive to pay both women at their required, matching rate. But that didn't happen. As a result, *both* women secured seats at the now more equitably set table.

You don't have to be a Hollywood star to share your privilege with others. There are plenty of smaller-scale ways to use whatever privilege you have to level the playing field or to help others navigate inequitable circumstances—and they cost you virtually nothing. One way to do this is by sharing information. When I started out as an independent consultant, I had no idea how much I should charge my clients. I had a friend and coworker who was a White man, and when I told him what I was planning on charging for an upcoming talk, he balked at the number. He told me the figure he would charge, which was considerably higher than what I quoted. The number was so high, in fact, that it made me uncomfortable. But I asked for it anyway, and, to my surprise and financial delight, I got it. My friend's transparency gave me the insight I needed to make sure I was valuing my work appropriately, and from then on, he became my go-to whenever I had to set fees.

Another way to use your privilege is by sharing access. Perhaps there's a leader pulling together a small team to lead a high-profile project. The leader knows you and your work very well, so you secure a spot on the team. This is the time to ask yourself: *Are there other people—particularly people of color—who also deserve to be on the team, but may not have been considered because they don't have the same casual relationship that you do with the leader?* Vouch for them! Use your access to secure a seat for someone else as well.

Sometimes sharing your privilege will mean you create another seat at the table, but other times you may need to give up your own seat to someone else. As someone who frequently attends conferences, I find it frustrating to see panel after panel made up exclusively of White speakers. But what's almost worse than that homogeneity is when someone *on* a panel—usually a White person—calls attention to the lack of diversity present and urges "us" to do better. The "us" they almost always refer to is some nebulous group—the conference organizers, the panel conveners, the attendees in the audience. But the reality is that *every single person* on that panel had an opportunity to change the panel's racial makeup. Rather than speaking up *during* the panel (which is a way of getting credit for calling out bad behavior while shirking all accountability), that panelist *could have* spoken up during the prep call when they first observed that all the panelists were White. They could have refused to participate unless the panel was diversified. They could even have offered for a person of color to take their place. This is where the theory of privilege meets practice. It's one thing to recognize that you've been given extra candy; it's another to take some of the candy out of your own trick-or-treat bag and give it to someone who has half as much candy as you do.

A common refrain I hear from clients I've worked with is "You broke me!" because they can't help but see racism everywhere now. While the feedback is typically delivered with a bit of a whining undertone and a desire to return to the rose-colored glasses of yesterday, I know this is really a moment to celebrate. What my clients experience as "breaking" is really a reprogramming: a process of eschewing old defaults and the inequities they perpetuate, and replacing them with something better.

CHAPTER 6

Decentering Whiteness

At this point in the book, you're likely on board with the truth that racism manifests in all forms and that our society is in dire need of correction. Once you see the White default, you can't unsee it. Once you recognize how a society systematically disenfranchises racial and ethnic minority groups, it becomes clear that a more equitable system would benefit everyone. So imagine walking into a boardroom or a classroom after reading this far in the book and being met with a question so seemingly simple, yet so loaded with history and layered with nuance: *"Why does diversity matter?"* To unpack the layers behind both the question and its answer, we must trace it back to a pivotal moment in 1978—a legal battle over affirmative action that would shape the modern narrative about diversity.

The *Regents of the University of California v. Bakke* case contested the legality of affirmative action in university admissions policies. At issue was a policy at the University of California, Davis, School of Medicine, that allocated sixteen of the one hundred available seats in each incoming class specifically for racial minority applicants. UC Davis had twice rejected Allan Bakke, the plaintiff in the case, and he sued on the grounds that the school's affirmative action policy was unconstitutional. Bakke argued that, were it not for the sixteen seats reserved for racial minority students, he would have been admitted (evidently, the other eighty-four seats that would likely go to White students did not provide sufficient opportunities for him). The California Supreme Court ruled in his favor, noting that the admissions policy violated the rights of White students, and the appeals process brought the case all the way to the United States Supreme Court.

As the justices weighed the cases brought by each side, they considered several "common-sense" rationales for why race might be allowable in admissions. These included: increasing the representation of historically underrepresented groups in medicine, countering systemic discrimination, increasing the population of doctors who could practice in underserved communities, and obtaining the educational benefits that flow from an ethnically diverse student body. The justices eschewed all these rationales—except for the final one. That is, in considering a range of reasons for why affirmative action practices would be necessary, arguments emphasizing the systemic injustices faced by people of color, the need to address the historical and ongoing underrepresentation of minorities, and the value of having more physicians who reflect underserved communities were deemed inadequate.

Instead, in the court's view, the only allowable reason for an affirmative action practice was that diversity led to a better educational experience for all. And the court didn't come to this conclusion on its own; an amicus brief submitted by four prestigious US universities (Columbia University, Harvard University, Stanford University, and the University of Pennsylvania) noted that "a primary value of liberal education should be exposure to new and provocative points of view...Minority students add such points of view, both in the classroom and in the larger university community."[1]

Ultimately, the court's decision seemed crafted as a compromise intended to appease both sides: The Supreme Court ruled that it *was* allowable to consider race in admissions but that UC Davis's program was a bridge too far. (Over forty years later, the practice of using race as a criterion in admissions decisions would ultimately be ruled unconstitutional in the 2023 *Students for Fair Admissions v. Harvard* and *Students for Fair Admissions v. University of North Carolina* cases.) The *Bakke* decision shaped not only the legal landscape but also the cultural conversation around affirmative action for years to come, lending legitimacy to the notion that affirmative action was appropriate *only* in cases where diversity would benefit the entire student body.

THE BUSINESS CASE FOR DIVERSITY

The court's concession that diversity did provide *some* benefits served as a kind of clarion call for the social scientists and diversity champions who reasoned that, if affirmative action would only be permitted on the basis that diversity benefits all, then it was up to them to prove that diversity was, indeed, a benefit to all. This led to a proliferation of studies highlighting the benefits of diversity on group decision-making, organizational dynamics, and the like.[2] Social science can be a powerful tool (indeed, other Supreme Court cases like *Brown v. Board of Education* were heavily influenced by research findings), so it makes sense that researchers were eager to provide definitive evidence of just how much better diversity made our world. In one such study, which is frequently cited as definitive evidence that diversity enhances critical thinking, participants were divided into groups of three.[3] Some groups were all White, while others were racially diverse—consisting of two White people and one person of color (an Asian, Black, or Hispanic participant). Each participant was given a packet of information containing forty-two clues about a homicide investigation: thirty clues that were identical for *all* the group partners, along with twelve clues that were unique to each group member. These three sets of a dozen unique clues were instrumental in solving the case, meaning that group members would have to effectively share information with one another in order to determine what really happened.

You might assume that the homogeneous groups shared information more freely—after all, if we're more comfortable around people of our own racial group, perhaps we're more comfortable sharing information with them, too. But that's not what happened. Instead, the all-White groups spent about four minutes less swapping information and deliberating on the case than their diverse counterparts did—a significant difference considering the groups had just thirty-five minutes to reach a conclusion. And when researchers instructed some groups to engage in a warm-up exercise in which they were to identify as many commonalities as possible (hobbies, experiences, favorite movies, and so on), the groups that spent time uncovering their similarities did *worse* on the subsequent murder mystery task than those who didn't draw attention to their similarities. This was the case no matter what the group's racial makeup was.

Ultimately, the study showed that groups whose members had a lot in common—whether those commonalities were visible traits like race, or superficial connections like a shared taste in movies—shared *less* information and made *poorer* decisions than diverse groups did. That's because participants in more diverse groups expected that the other members of their group would have access to different information and hold a range of perspectives. This (correct) assumption prompted more thorough discussions of the case and enabled them to uncover the key details necessary to arrive at the correct conclusion. Groups that were more homogeneous, on the other hand, erroneously believed they were alike in other ways as well (including taking for granted that the information in their packets was the same). As a result, they devoted less time to seeking out those differences, which undermined their ability to collaborate and make decisions effectively.

That influential study had *proven* that diverse teams shared more information and made better decisions than homogeneous ones did, contributing to the mounting evidence that diverse teams produced more creative and accurate solutions to problems, deliberated more thoroughly when it came to complex topics, and so on.[4] Nearly a decade after the murder mystery study was published, the evidence that diversity was good for us was pervasive—so much so that a 2014 issue of *Scientific American*, "How Diversity Empowers Science and Innovation," was dedicated to the topic.[5] (Katherine W. Phillips authored one of the issue's articles, "How Diversity Makes Us Smarter."[6]) This was a sign of meaningful progress! After decades of reticent grumblings about affirmative action policies, many institutions of higher education were *finally* accepting that fostering diversity in their student bodies and workforces was a worthy goal.

Corporations became the next battleground, and consumers and employees began pressuring companies to diversify their ranks. At first, business leaders were largely skeptical. Even after Google became one of the first companies to publicly share diversity data in 2014, many other tech companies grappled with whether to follow suit. It became clear that leaders would only make changes if there was proof that doing so would positively impact their bottom line.

Taking a page from the ideological fight in higher education, advocates for diversity leveraged the ample research showing that diverse teams foster stronger collaboration, drive innovation, and enhance problem-solving—framing their argument in a way that resonated with these leaders. Bolstered by research demonstrating that organizations led by more diverse teams experience better financial outcomes than those with more homogeneous leadership,[7] the "business case for diversity," as it became known, essentially made the argument that diversity positively impacts a company's earnings.

By 2017, academic institutions, public companies, and even political candidates (at least, some of them) were talking about why diversity was important. As a DEI practitioner, I suppose I should've been happy that diversity had gone mainstream. But my excitement was tempered by my conflicted feelings around the increasingly ubiquitous "business case for diversity" narrative. I was baffled by the fact that a (White, often male) company leader could examine their employee demographics and clearly observe that, for instance, only 2 percent of their workforce was Black, 0.5 percent was Indigenous / Native American, and 4 percent was Hispanic or Latino, and *not* wonder how those paltry numbers were affecting their underrepresented employees' well-being. But I was even *more* perplexed by the fact that the best justification the industry had come up with for why people of color needed greater representation was that our presence would make *White* people more effective at their jobs, thereby making more money for the company. It felt off to me, but I couldn't find the words to articulate why that was the case. Nor could I conceive of how to answer the "Why should we care about diversity?" question in a way that would address my moral conundrum while also seeming compelling to business leaders.

And then I encountered some new research by Dr. Vicky Plaut—a well-known social psychologist and professor at UC Berkeley School of Law—and her graduate student Kynesha-wau Hurd that connected so many dots that it felt like my brain might short-circuit.[8] The provocative question at the heart of their research—"Does Diversity-Benefits Ideology Undermine Inclusion?"—was exactly what I myself had been wondering.[9]

The "business case for diversity" was positive in many ways. It shone a light on the lack of meaningful diversity within many organizations and gave companies a clear incentive to hire racial minorities. The problem was that it became the *singular* narrative for why diversity was important—a narrative that centered entirely on the (mostly White) organizations and leaders doing the hiring. In other words, as Hurd and Plaut asserted, the prevailing narrative concerning "the benefits of diversity" positioned *White* people as the beneficiary. This posed a problem, they argued, because if White people entered diverse environments expecting to gain something from the experience, it would foster a mentality they referred to as "entitlement to diversity." Hurd and Plaut reasoned that White people might approach diverse spaces solely as a means to their own ends (i.e., opportunities to make more money for—and from—their now-more-innovative-and-lucrative companies) while failing to consider the experiences of people of color, or their own impact on the experiences of people of color, within those settings. In their view, this business case for diversity would reinforce existing power structures that centered White priorities—even as it appeared to advocate for racial equity.

In addition, Hurd and Plaut contended that what those oft-cited findings indicating that "all" people benefited from diversity actually demonstrated was that White individuals gained the most from diverse environments. (Indeed, that research had little or nothing to say about the impact of diversity on people of color.) Taken together, the existing conversation about "the benefits of diversity" risked *reinforcing* systemic racial inequity instead of dismantling it. It encouraged White people to support diversity initiatives without having to acknowledge—or address—the underlying cause of underrepresentation: racism.

Take, for example, the murder mystery study. Unquestionably, the White participants made better decisions when working within a more diverse group. But given the design of the study, we *just don't know* if the same was true for participants of color. Would their outcomes have been different if they, too, had been placed in a homogeneous (i.e., all-Asian, all-Black, or all-Hispanic) group, rather than a diverse one? Moreover, the study revealed nothing about what the group experience was like for participants of color. Were their contributions to the discussion received as warmly as those from their White counterparts, or were they marginalized (as is often the case for people of color in diverse settings)? Did they ultimately play a greater role in their groups' correct conclusions—perhaps because minority participants were more experienced in navigating differences and communicating effectively—than Phillips's study accounted for? We don't know—because the study focused solely on homogeneity and difference with White participants as its reference point.

With this renewed perspective, I couldn't help but reflect on my experiences as a graduate student, and later as a post-doctoral fellow, at two predominantly White institutions: Indiana University and Purdue University. While developing a diversity and inclusion orientation program for the incoming first-year class, I often heard from faculty and administrators that for many students—most of whom came from predominantly White towns in Indiana—Purdue would be the most diverse environment they'd ever encountered. They highlighted the advantages that these students would gain by "finally" meeting a Black person—possibly through being assigned as roommates in their freshman year or by working together on a class project. Even then, I couldn't shake the thought that the "benefit" in that scenario wouldn't be shared equally. I'd heard far too many stories from Black students about what it was like to *be* the first Black person their peers had ever had meaningful contact with—an experience that was often isolating, exhausting, and filled with the unspoken pressure to educate others while navigating their own sense of belonging. Later, in my corporate career, I heard similar experiences from people of color who often felt like museum exhibits—observed with curiosity by their White colleagues, who were eager to learn but hesitant to engage fully.

So when Drs. Hurd and Plaut outlined the risks of the widespread "diversity benefits everyone" rhetoric, they pinpointed the root issue of something I had experienced firsthand, heard about repeatedly, and long felt uneasy about. What I *hadn't* considered was that, as a social psychologist, I was perpetuating the issue by publishing research that inadvertently—and sometimes explicitly—supported a message that a set of conditions was "beneficial" so long as it served the interests of White people. All of those studies on the benefits of diversity for corporations could have positioned people of color as central beneficiaries of diversity practices. They *could have* highlighted how expanding access to larger, more diverse talent pools increases the likelihood that high-performing but historically underrepresented minorities are recognized and hired. They *could have* addressed the fact that overtly discriminatory hiring practices long confined people of color to lower-paying, less-prestigious roles—and that companies today bear a responsibility to acknowledge and correct for this legacy of disenfranchisement. They *could have* shown that when leadership teams are more diverse, it challenges ingrained biases by normalizing the presence of individuals who don't fit the "typical" profile in high-ranking positions, eroding the assumption that only certain groups are naturally suited for power and influence. They *could have* emphasized that countless innovations have emerged from frequently marginalized individuals (people of color, mothers, disabled people) who reached a breaking point and turned their frustration into groundbreaking solutions that mainstream industries had overlooked. Any of these arguments would have begun to place people of color at the center of the "who benefits from diversity" discussion.

But the most-cited reports didn't highlight these things. Much like the Supreme Court, which sidestepped historic and current racial inequities in favor of emphasizing the benefits that (White) students gained from exposure to diversity, "the business case" for diversity celebrated the inclusion of marginalized groups primarily for how they enriched (White, male) employees' and leaders' organizational outcomes. There was no assessment of whether the resulting "advantages" of innovation, better decision-making, or increased company revenue would compensate for the costs incurred by people of color.

Drs. Hurd and Plaut reached a logical conclusion: If people of color gained no advantages from those diverse settings, their inclusion was superficial at best. At worst, their inclusion reinforced existing racial hierarchies in which White people get to dictate the terms of who does (or *doesn't*) gain entry or access—all while fooling themselves into believing they're championing a policy of equality.

I felt convicted: If we were going to make real strides in combating systemic racial inequity, we—DEI practitioners, social scientists, and all those leading in this space—would have to stop acting as though curating a world that catered to White people's sensibilities, apprehensions, and desires would necessarily yield equity for all. And when I transitioned from higher education into corporate DEI as a consultant at Paradigm, I had my first opportunity to meaningfully change that narrative.

BUILDING A NEW "CASE"
FOR DIVERSITY

When I joined Paradigm in 2019, I saw the same warning signs of "diversity entitlement" that Drs. Hurd and Plaut had raised alarms about in their research. Our clients were eager to bring us in to talk about the importance of combating bias and why diversity was important, but they *also* warned us about the fine line we would have to walk. We were peppered with questions about how we would deal with skeptics and how to convince managers to "let" their team members take two hours out of their busy workdays to attend a DEI presentation. Though they didn't say it this overtly, what our clients were really getting at was this: *"Some members of our company [the White people, the men] will be resistant to this content, so you'll need to get their buy-in early by showing what's in it for them."*

As I prepared for my first workshop, I found myself reviewing slides that led with "the business case" as the reason our audience should care about our message that day.

With Hurd and Plaut's cautionary words echoing in my mind, I put myself in the position of a person of color who would attend our workshop. I considered how they would feel when they heard *me*, their (Black) unconscious bias workshop facilitator, say that their inclusion in the company was largely about driving profits. I reflected on how they likely *already* felt overlooked in meetings and sidelined for promotions, only to be showcased as a token representative when the company sought to demonstrate its commitment to diversity. This perspective helped me remember that the skeptical White attendees weren't the only people in our audience— nor were they the only people we needed to win over within the first ten minutes of the presentation. We wanted the people of color in the audience to feel invested in the rest of the workshop—*not* disengage because the presentation seemed unconnected to, or unconcerned with, their experiences.

Emboldened by these realizations, I advocated for the addition of a slide focused on the "moral case" for diversity. That slide had a straightforward message: Caring about (and investing in) DEI is simply the right thing to do. I drew attention to statistics regarding the underrepresentation of women and people of color in corporate settings. I cited research on the harm that people from historically and currently marginalized groups experience when we're the only one like us in the room. I noted that organizations that claim to champion diversity while failing to create environments where everyone can thrive are ultimately working against their own goals.

I suggested that instead of viewing people of color as props to support White employees or enrich White organizations, companies that authentically advocated for diversity would allocate considerable resources toward nurturing employees of color, ensuring they had the tools to thrive. In one of my proudest moments, I typed the following words into the speaker notes that would become the script for all facilitators: "Allowing an environment that is toxic to a certain subset of people to exist isn't just bad for business. It's *wrong*."

Did I *also* share the research showing that more diverse teams financially outperformed homogeneous ones? Absolutely! But was that *really* the most compelling rationale we could offer for why the corporate world needed to cease being predominantly White and male, rife with micro- and macro-aggressions against women and people of color? Absolutely not! In my view, the fact that acting ethically also benefited the bottom line was icing on the cake, but—and this was critical—*even if "doing diversity" was bad for business, I would advocate for it anyway.*

In hindsight, this addendum to the presentation doesn't sound so radical, but it *was* at the time. My client had already signed off on the previous iteration of the workshop, and I—barely a month on the job and brand-new to this client relationship—was proposing a small but potentially controversial revision. It took some persuading, but in the end, I succeeded not only in altering the content of this client's workshop but also in reshaping how all Paradigm facilitators approached both the business *and* moral arguments for diversity.

If we want to make diverse spaces that truly benefit everyone, we must first adjust the narrative around *why* those spaces are valuable. Telling White people that they would benefit from diversity effectively fostered the belief that people of color were there chiefly—or exclusively—to facilitate *White* people's learning, to serve them in some way. Moreover, if we operate under the assumption that White people's professional success or general benefit is a prerequisite for racial equity, our justifications for pursuing this work will fall short of serving its true beneficiaries.

"The benefits of diversity," and "the business case" that they spawned, reinforced a familiar narrative in our society: one that places White people at the top of the social hierarchy and prioritizes their physical and psychological needs—often at the expense of people of color. And an approach that subjugates the needs of people of color cannot possibly yield equal benefits for them. White people are equal participants in diverse spaces—just as responsible for the impact they have on others (including the harm they may cause) as they are for what benefits they reap from those environments. In many cases, their needs can be weighed equally with the needs of people of color. However, because the roots of systemic racial inequity run deep, and because creating racial equity often requires substantial intervention, sometimes people of color will need to be the *only* priority—and White people's needs may not be considered at all.

NOT EVERY PLACE NEEDS TO BE
DESIGNED FOR WHITE PEOPLE

"How many White people does it take to make a space White?" my colleague Anna asked our group of allyship workshop participants.[10] While it sounded like the setup to a bad joke, it was an earnest question she had grappled with for some time. Several years earlier, Anna had participated in a yoga certification workshop led by a woman of color and attended by a racially and ethnically diverse group of students. The instructor had posed this very question to the group, and one person—also a woman of color—raised her hand and delivered a simple answer:

"One."

For Anna, a boisterous White woman with a vibrant personality (and a talkative nature that rivaled my own), this response was a real revelation. As she recounted her experience to the allyship group, Anna shared how she had struggled with the awareness that her very presence might compromise the safe and inclusive environment the workshop had promised for other participants. She recognized that the women of color in her workshop likely navigated many predominantly White spaces, and that they might need sanctuary from the requirements of those spaces so they could comfortably and vulnerably express their identities and share their experiences without explaining themselves or altering their behaviors to accommodate White people. And she could understand how the presence of even one White person could compel the women of color to modify the stories or jokes they told (to ensure Anna understood their references), justify their interpretations of the microaggressions they faced (in case Anna—like many other White people—dismissed them as complainers), or withdraw entirely.

Anna considered her options. Though she ultimately decided not to quit the certification workshop, for the remainder of the session she did everything she could not to suck up all (or *any*) of the oxygen in the room. When the instructor posed a question to the group, she hesitated, giving others a chance to respond before raising her hand to contribute. During breaks, she lingered at the edges of the small groups forming in the space, waiting for someone to invite her into the conversation rather than inserting herself as was her typical practice. Instead of taking offense to the revelation that her presence as a White person fundamentally altered the space, Anna took it seriously. Instead of centering and prioritizing her own feelings, Anna centered the feelings of the other attendees, committing to find ways to make her presence—and her Whiteness—less conspicuous or commanding.[11]

When Anna first shared this story, I was surprised. Not because of how the woman of color answered the question—my experience, too, is that it only takes one White person to make a space White—but because of how Anna responded. Anna, and some of my other collaborators in the DEI space, often spoke of the importance of "decentering Whiteness." While I certainly didn't object to the concept, I had always struggled to integrate that phrase into my own daily language. I knew what "centering Whiteness" *felt* like—it felt like adjusting my language (code-switching) to ensure the White people in the room understood what I was saying, or circling back to explain a (Black) cultural reference that fell flat, for example. "*De*centering Whiteness" felt like one of those buzzwords that had a nice ring to it, but I found it challenging to explain to White people what it *meant*—likely because most of my clients were White people accustomed to operating in White spaces. They'd never been forced to notice that the spaces they inhabited—even the relatively racially diverse ones like their workplaces—were fundamentally designed to accommodate them.

While *I* appreciated Anna's story, I could tell from their reactions that it unsettled many of our workshop participants. "What did she *mean* when she said it only takes one White person to make a White space?" one scoffed. Another chimed in: "I mean, what does a 'White space' even *mean*?" Their proverbial hackles were raised, prepared to defend Anna's unwavering right to exist in whatever space she wanted.

I was accustomed to encountering this kind of resistance. I often worked with companies poised to launch employee resource groups (ERGs), affinity groups for people who share identities that are underrepresented in the workplace and/or marginalized in society, such as racial or ethnic minorities and members of the LGBTQ+

community. Inevitably, as my client prepared to roll out their ERG program, they would ask me: "How do we explain to people that there won't be an all-male or all-White ERG?" The first time I heard the question I had to choke back laughter. Wasn't it obvious that the *entire company*, with its mostly White, mostly male employees, was the de facto White/male ERG?[12] The sole intention behind forming those groups was to connect individuals from underrepresented demographics and provide them with safe, supportive spaces—spaces that White employees already had by default. After the same question was posed a second, third, and fourth time, I stopped laughing. I discovered that my clients' concerns about reverse-racism allegations were, regrettably, rooted in reality: They recounted remarks from teammates such as "Oh, so *they* can have a Black-only group, but *we* can't have a White-only group? That certainly doesn't sound 'inclusive' to me."

To foster collaboration in diverse environments, White people must let go of the belief that every space should be tailored to them. Yes, this may mean that there are some places White people just don't need to be. Part of "not doing harm" in diverse spaces is learning to discern if, and when, your presence as a White person is necessary or desired. Unfortunately, the individuals opposed to ERGs had internalized the notion that diversity efforts *must* include them. In their minds, if an initiative didn't include them—much less welcome them—then it wasn't a worthwhile endeavor.

This insular thinking has implications beyond affinity groups. Once, a company I partnered with was examining their talent pipeline and discovered that employees of color were less likely to advance beyond middle management than their White employees were. After conducting some focus groups, we discovered that this disparity was due to a mentorship gap: While White employees had more (White) senior leaders at the company who could shepherd them into the next stages of their career, employees of color lacked that same guidance. This was a problem that had a relatively simple solution: Identify opportunities to connect employees of color with mentors who could help them advance their careers. And that's exactly what the company did. Shortly thereafter, the team received a disheartening message from Legal: A mentorship program tailored specifically to employees of color could expose the company to potential discrimination claims. Legal feared that if White employees learned about the program, they might view it as "special treatment" for employees of color and raise objections about White exclusion. After much back-and-forth, it became evident that we had two choices: Open the mentorship program up to all employees or abandon it altogether.

Ultimately, the company chose to retain the program—the need for mentorship among employees of color was, after all, still pressing—and modified the criteria to allow *any* employee in the designated leadership-track roles to participate. Of course, there were workarounds: The team overseeing the program did intentional outreach to ERGs serving the company's racial/ethnic minority employees and crafted the invitation to emphasize that this was an initiative to help increase diversity in leadership roles at the company. Even so, the message was received loud and clear: There wasn't room for employees of color to have something uniquely their own, and if the initiative didn't also help White employees advance to senior leadership—despite clear data showing they already dominated those roles—it shouldn't be implemented at all.

I objected to this line of thinking then, and I still object to it now. Sometimes addressing the needs of people of color *will* call for initiatives designed specifically—and exclusively—for them. (Remember that the whole reason for such initiatives is to address and rectify the systemic inequities people of color have endured for ages.) Sometimes the needs of White people may call for a tailored initiative as well. And sometimes we can simultaneously support multiple groups with the same initiative. But we must resist the urge to view issues through the lens of White people *first* and make decisions based on that orientation. As a comprehensive approach, diversity does yield advantages that can benefit everyone—but it may not be feasible to realize all those benefits for every group at once.

Curators of diverse environments need to acknowledge the distinct needs and viewpoints of both White people and people of color and address them accordingly. And there are times when addressing these needs separately is not only necessary but also beneficial for everyone involved. A clear example of this comes from a company that organized small-group discussions following an anti-racism workshop. Creating separate groups for White employees and employees of color ended up being very beneficial for the discussion, because it meant that White people could share their raw thoughts without fear of being judged for admissions of ignorance, calls for accountability from their peers, or the pressure of "getting it right" in front of people of color. Conversely, people of color could openly share *their* unfiltered thoughts—whether it was relief that the topic was finally being addressed at work, frustration that it had taken this long, or their hopes for what true racial equity could look like—without fear of being labeled "complainers" or "radicals," or facing other forms of judgment from their White colleagues. While this kind of separation won't work for every organization (those who choose this path must be prepared to defend it), it's one way to cultivate conversations that will yield benefits for most, if not all, participants.

By the same token, curators of diverse environments also need to establish guardrails that mitigate the harm that's possible when people from different backgrounds, experiences, and perspectives come together with their clashing viewpoints and perspectives. One of my favorite ways to do this is by creating a set of norms for how a group will engage with one another. Whether they're called values, community agreements, or something else, these norms make clear for everyone what behavior is accepted and what behavior is not—including what will happen if they don't comply. For example, having a group norm to share airtime is good, but even *better* is letting people know that folks who've spoken up multiple times will be interrupted with a gentle, "We've heard a lot from you, Evelyn. Let's give others a chance to chime in." Finally, codifying these norms is a great way for groups to showcase their values and personality. For example, a group I worked with once was struggling to find a balance between addressing potentially harmful comments and offering grace to those still learning how to navigate a diverse environment. They ended up landing on a simple safe word: *pause.* Any time someone said or did something that made another person in the group feel uncomfortable, that person could interject with "Pause!" This gave the speaker immediate feedback, allowed the other person a simple way to call them out, and gave everyone a chance at a do-over. (Other clients have used fun variations on this idea, using call-and-response phrases like "Hold up!" and "Let me try again," or "Ouch" and "Oops.") Group agreements are useful in lots of situations—when you're bringing together a new team at work, hosting a social gathering (my book club has group agreements!), or visiting an online forum, for example—and taking the time to create them highlights for all participants that diverse learning environments require accountability and psychological safety.

SOME STUFF JUST *ISN'T* FOR WHITE PEOPLE

Decentering Whiteness isn't just about understanding and respecting the physical spaces that you, as an individual, should not enter. It also requires an awareness of the cultural spaces that must remain off-limits.

I was a child of the 1990s and early 2000s, and I'm still convinced that those years produced some of the finest music ever made. Ours was an era of boy bands, girl groups, rap songs with infectious refrains that permeated pop culture ("mo' money, mo' problems," anyone?), and moderately priced concerts that we could actually afford to attend. The summer of 2005, just before my senior year of high school, brought with it the song "Gold Digger," which would become one of the most unforgettable songs in music history. The song sampled Ray Charles's "I Got a Woman" featuring vocals by Jamie Foxx, and the chorus had a simple yet memorable end rhyme: "Now I ain't sayin' she a gold digger, / but she ain't messing with no broke..." The radio edits of the song always trailed off, but those of us with the album—or with any sense of rhyme—knew *exactly* what word had been omitted.

The summer anthem that I relished bopping along to in the car with my Black friends became a source of strife as the school year began. Whether I was at a homecoming dance or a post-football-game party, "Gold Digger" was a staple on the playlist. And without fail, every time that censored line was about to drop, I'd hold my breath. My experience until then had taught me that most people my age (or *any* age, for that matter) knew that the N-word was reserved for use exclusively by Black people, if it was going to be used at all. But the universal appeal of the song seemed to serve as an open invitation for White people to relax their verbal inhibitions. More than a handful of times, I'd be listening to the song (radio edit or no) in mixed company only to hear someone who was definitely not Black belting out the full chorus—N-word and all. Any protestation on my part, or on the part of my Black friends, was met with the same retort: "If *you* can say it, why can't *I*?" The short answer that I wished I'd had the courage to say at that age was: "Because I'm Black and you're not. The end." (The long answer, of course, is that many Black people have chosen to reclaim the N-word as a form of empowerment after a long history of White people wielding it against them as a derogatory term to dehumanize and oppress them. The Black folks who use it today do so to subvert its negative connotations and express defiance against a legacy of injustice. But when *White* people use it? It still carries the historical weight of racism and violence.) As I matured and engaged in more racially diverse environments, I became familiar with that same entitled sentiment. (Perhaps those teens who insisted on singing the N-word grew up to be the very adults who objected to the formation of minority-focused ERGs.)

One challenge of inhabiting diverse spaces is that we will inevitably encounter information, customs, and language that aren't really meant for broader audiences at all. Put bluntly,

some stuff just *isn't* for White people. The N-word is probably a straightforward example to most—but even White people who understand that the N-word is off-limits may find it
challenging to discern in more nuanced situations when they
can *engage* and when they should simply *observe.*

When I was in college, my sorority (Alpha Kappa Alpha
Sorority, Incorporated, Gamma Chi chapter, in case anyone
was wondering) was the undisputed champion of stepping—
a dance form commonly practiced by historically Black
fraternities and sororities. Every year, our chapter choreo-
graphed rhythmically complex, visually captivating routines
that won over the judges of our annual campus step show,
GreekScene. Despite our success, stepping was predominantly
perceived as "just a Black thing," and few people outside of
the Black community were familiar with it. So when it was
announced that Coca-Cola would be hosting the *Sprite Step
Off,* a national, televised stepping competition that spanned
twenty cities and featured a pool of $1.5 million in prize
money, we were ecstatic.[13] Stepping was going *mainstream!*

That first year of the competition was not without contro-
versy. After it concluded, all anyone could talk about was the
team that had been crowned the winner: the Arkansas chapter of Zeta Tau Alpha (ZTA), an all-White sorority. Feelings
were . . . complicated.[14] Some people accused ZTA of cultural
appropriation, claiming they had no right to participate in
the stepping tradition rooted in Black culture. Others noted
that the sorority had learned the art of stepping under the
mentorship of the Black sororities and fraternities on their

campus as part of an initiative to encourage Greek unity—the White folks were simply honoring this rich tradition. There seemed to be only two sides: Either White people shouldn't step (and then Black people shouldn't be upset if such traditions remained marginalized), or Black people had to come to terms with the fact that White people stepping—and even outperforming Black participants in stepping competitions—was a condition of a more diverse and inclusive society in which Black cultural traditions became mainstream. There seemed to be no easy answers.

Having had more than ten years to reflect on this debate, I now understand that this imposed binary was unjust. Characterizing ZTA's actions as malicious cultural appropriation was unfair to them, yet it was equally unfair that the price of acknowledging Black traditions meant they could be freely adopted by anyone.[15] The crucial third perspective I wish I'd been able to articulate back then is that the White women of ZTA should have acknowledged that their *ability* to enter the competition didn't imply their *entitlement* to do so. Like Anna in her yoga workshop, rather than assuming their ability to step qualified them for the competition, they could have paused to reflect, *"Is it* appropriate *for us to enter this competition?"* With *this* perspective, they might have realized that they were guests in the realm of stepping; showcasing their skills in a step show on their campus was one thing, but competing for prize money on a national stage was something entirely different. Of course, this isn't a level of discernment I'd expect from a group of college-age women presented with an opportunity to win a $100,000 scholarship check. But it *is* the level of discernment required *now* of White people who want to learn how to exist collaboratively in diverse spaces. In a toss-up between observer and participant, if there's any hesitation at all, stay on the sidelines.

Years ago, I began a running joke that one day I would write a book called "The Art of Telling White People No."[16] I was convinced that White people's entitlement—not just the diversity entitlement that Hurd and Plaut spoke of, but entitlement to any space, any language, and any custom—was the ultimate obstacle to an equitable society. And I believed if I could just change that by helping White people learn how to take no for an answer without seeking justification or an explanation, I could change the world.

I maintain this belief. In earlier chapters, I dedicated considerable attention to the mindset shifts necessary for recognizing bias and exploring the new perspectives that emerge from more accurate bias detection. But what happens once the proverbial scales have fallen from your eyes? *It's time to behave differently.* And that means removing the implicit (or explicit!) sense of entitlement to exist in the world without consideration of others. It involves embracing a new role as collaborator—and sometimes only as observer—in a diverse environment, rather than positioning yourself as its central figure. It means taking no for an answer. And ideally, it means learning to tell *yourself* no—as in, opting out of the stepping competition, buying tickets to the event, and cheering your Black fellow students on.

This is the work of existing as a White person in diverse spaces. And yet, as we've seen, the reality is that many White people *do* exist in exclusively White spaces. This means that the biggest opportunity for impact may not necessarily be in changing how you engage with people of color, but in changing how you engage with other White people. This requires disrupting norms about how to communicate, diving headfirst into uncomfortable territory, and holding people accountable for things they may not even know are a problem. On that front alone, there's plenty of work to do.

CHAPTER 7

The Subtle Art of Calling Out Bias

My love for the television series *Scandal* ran deep: For six straight years, from 2012 to 2018, I cleared my calendar on Thursdays at 9 p.m. to watch it. There was something special about watching a fast-talking, whip-smart, impeccably dressed Black woman rally her misfit gang of "gladiators in suits" to solve her powerful clients' most pressing problems. (Even my mom knew that *Scandal* time was untouchable, and she never called when it was on.) Having been an intermittent viewer of *Grey's Anatomy*, I was no stranger to creator Shonda Rhimes's signature style. But *Scandal* pushed boundaries even Rhimes had set herself—especially when it came to sex on network TV.

By the time Rhimes's next series, *How to Get Away with Murder*, aired in 2014, fans had come to expect her high-stakes storytelling and explicit sexual overtones—but some were unprepared for depictions of same-sex intimacy. Granted, *Scandal* had featured a sex scene between two men—but *How to Get Away with Murder* pushed the envelope even further, granting its gay male characters the freedom of promiscuity and sexual variety that Rhimes's heterosexual couples had always enjoyed on-screen.

How to Get Away with Murder premiered to rave reviews, but its particular depiction of gay sex proved too much for some viewers. While Shonda Rhimes faced a flood of backlash on Twitter after the premiere, I found myself locked in my own online confrontation over the show. That week, as the Thursday-night programming ended, I scrolled through Facebook and paused at a disheartening post: A childhood friend, Tracy, had posted a paragraphs-long rant declaring that she would no longer support Shonda Rhimes's shows after watching that night's episode.[1] She was, evidently, gravely offended by the erosion of on-screen modesty and questioned whether the sex scene between two men she'd just witnessed was *really* the kind of content we wanted to show our children. I read the post and scoffed at her hypocrisy. Tracy was a *Scandal* lover just like me, and she had never objected to the fact that the story at the show's center was, after all, a steamy, seasons-long extramarital affair. More-over, I doubted that anyone's impressionable young children (including hers) were watching the show: *How to Get Away with Murder* had a TV-14 rating—in part because it also featured a lot of violence—and aired at 10 p.m. But Tracy didn't seem upset about the scenes in which people were bludgeoned over the head or bloody corpses flashed across the screen. I knew her sudden indignation wasn't just about the explicit nature of the sex depicted on the show. She was moved to clutch her proverbial pearls because the sex scene featured *two men*.

I let out an exasperated sigh and scrolled on, but I couldn't shake the frustration her post had stirred in me. Thirty minutes later, I was pulling it up once again so I could read it word for word to my partner. I needed someone to echo my outrage and to confirm that Tracy's stance was, without question, homophobic. He provided the validation I was looking for, and, feeling self-satisfied, we agreed that such closed-minded comments were not worth any more of our time. I put down my phone and prepared to call it a night.

Yet the unsettling sensation in my stomach persisted, signaling that something in me was still unresolved. What lingered was the realization of my *own* hypocrisy: I wasn't addressing my friend's homophobic comments in the way I knew—and often advised others—was the right way to confront bias. At the time, I was fully engaged in research on this very topic, and all available evidence was pointing to an undeniable conclusion: If you want to stop biased behavior, *you must call out the person responsible for the behavior.* Tracy had no idea that I'd spent thirty minutes quietly seething over her post, offended on behalf of any gay man who might read it. If I wanted to encourage her to recognize the homophobic double standard informing her commentary, I would have to say something to her.

It would have been very easy to convince myself that while Tracy's bias needed to be called out, *I* didn't have to be the person to do it. But to sit back and hope that someone else would read her post and feel compelled to speak up would be to fall prey to the bystander effect, a paradoxical phenomenon wherein the more people there are to witness a troubling event, the *less* likely the event is to be reported.[2] Plus, emerging research at the time was showing that people outside a marginalized group did not face the same social repercussions for calling out bias as did those within it.[3] In other words, because I was not part of the LGBTQ+ community, my words might be received more openly than if they had come from a gay person.

Knowing what I needed to do didn't make executing it any simpler. I spent the next thirty minutes furiously typing on my phone's keyboard, crafting a lengthy, multi-paragraph reply. I pointed out Tracy's double standard. I asked where her outrage had been during the similarly explicit hetero sex scenes in the other shows we watched and loved. I reminded her that we, as Black people, were quite familiar with the problem of underrepresentation in the media, and that if *we* deserved representation that reflected the fullness of who we were, then gay men deserved that as well.

Feeling satisfied with my response, I hovered my thumb over the post button, but just before I went to press it, I was struck by hesitation once again. *This* time I wrestled with whether to send the response privately to my friend or engage in the discussion publicly by posting it as a comment. Again, I relied on the research, which showed that public confrontations of bias can have a positive impact on the behavior of the person in question *and* on the behavior of those who observe the confrontation. I knew that calling Tracy out publicly might embarrass her, making her defensive or unwilling to engage. But I saw that as a risk worth taking. A private message could encourage her to reconsider her perspective, yes; but a *public* conversation had the potential to do that while also reaching others in her circle who might share her views.[4]

By this point, it was very late, and I knew I wouldn't be able to sleep without saying *something*—the sense of urgency in my body ran too deep. Ultimately, I condensed my argument and posted my reply publicly on her original post: Tracy was being homophobic, her comments revealed a troubling double standard, and I did not agree. I was agitated by the entire experience—but that uncomfortable feeling in the pit of my stomach was gone. I'd responded in alignment with my values by calling out harmful rhetoric and reinforcing the importance of accountability. I would not have my silence— even on a cluttered social feed—mistaken for agreement.

In the wake of that experience, I became consumed with learning about how other people called out and challenged bias when the opportunity presented itself. As I pored over the literature on the topic, I came across some statistics that left me feeling discouraged and disheartened. In one study, participants were asked to reflect on biased comments they'd recently encountered: who made the remark (e.g., a friend or stranger), where it occurred (e.g., a dorm or classroom), how it made them feel, and how they chose to respond.[5] These comments (most often made by friends or acquaintances in private settings) went largely unchallenged. At first, I was incensed that only 33.9 percent of participants in the study confronted the bias they witnessed. Most people, it seemed, didn't live up to the egalitarian values they allegedly endorsed. But the more I reflected on the data, the more it became clear: If someone like me—equipped with theoretical knowledge, trained in addressing bias, and dedicated to studying it as a profession and a calling—found it difficult to speak up in the moment, then how much harder must it be for "the average person"? This raised a crucial question: *What*, if anything, can we do to overcome this widespread reluctance to speak up?

CALLING OUT BIAS CHANGES BEHAVIOR (NO MATTER *HOW* YOU CALL IT OUT)

Research suggests that the primary reasons people hesitate to challenge racial bias are not knowing *what* to say, *how* to say it, or whether speaking up will make any difference at all.[6] (I felt the weight of those first two uncertainties during my Facebook engagement with Tracy.) Of course, these three categories—*what*, *how*, and *whether*—betray the full complexity of why any one person would hesitate to call out bias in a given encounter. One person may be concerned about appearing preachy, self-righteous, or judgmental; another may be more concerned with sparing the other person's feelings, not wanting to embarrass them or make them feel guilty; yet another may simply fear confrontation—will the other person explode in outrage in response? Another person may fear being brushed off, while another might not be willing to risk the potential damage to the relationship.

Sometimes, there are also power dynamics to consider: Calling out a peer for their bias is one thing, but confronting a boss or mentor comes with not only interpersonal consequences but also fears of retaliation, job loss, and other professional repercussions.[7] Human beings are built for connection with others; even if you *know* you are morally right, being isolated from friends and loved ones can be lonely. Ultimately, the question of whether speaking up will make any difference at all could come down to a cost-benefit analysis: *"Is confronting this person worth it?"* It could also be shaped by a person's prior experiences: *"The last time I tried to call out behavior like this, the person dismissed me and carried on as if nothing happened."*

The choices people make about whether to confront bias or to stay silent are complex and nuanced. But over the years, my investigations into the topic, which became the central theme of my postdoctoral research at Purdue, crystallized around a simple truth: *Confronting bias in any way creates meaningful change* (maybe not all the time, but often enough to be significant). If your goal is to interrupt a person's harmful behavior, saying something—*anything!*—is better than saying nothing at all. Rolling your eyes? That counts! Saying "Not cool, dude," and walking away? Also good! Commenting on a Facebook post (even if drafting it takes the better part of your evening, as it did in my case)? Definitely preferable to silence. What's vital is that you voice your disapproval and make it clear that the person's words or behaviors aren't acceptable.

Indeed, one study provided compelling evidence that the precise words a person uses when calling out bias don't matter much for immediate behavior change.[8] In this study, White participants were told they would participate in a brief online conversation with another person, then join forces to complete an inference task. During the online conversation, the person they were chatting with (who was actually a member of the research team pretending to be a participant in the study) would share some information about their personal life, their hobbies, and their race—which was always White.

Once the online conversation was completed, participants were presented with a set of images featuring Black and White individuals, accompanied by brief one-sentence "job descriptions." Their task was to pair a description with each individual by inferring their occupation. In most cases, the descriptions and their inferred professions were neutral—for instance, *"This person works with numbers"* could describe an accountant or a math teacher. But in three critical rounds, the participants were shown pictures of Black people accompanied by descriptors that were meant to invite stereotyping. *"This person depends on the government for money"* could describe someone on welfare (responses that would be consistent with stereotypes about Black people), *or* it could describe a federal employee (a non-stereotypic response). *"This person can be found behind bars"* might describe a criminal, but it could also describe a bartender. And finally, *"This person can be found wandering the streets"* could describe a homeless person, but it could also describe a tourist. If this feels a bit like a trap, that's because it was—and a reliable one. Out of 121 participants, only 2 people avoided providing any stereotypic responses; most people (83.5 percent) gave at least two.

This gave the "other participant" (who, remember, was working with the researchers) a great opportunity to call out the White participants' bias—which they did, sticking close to one of two scripts. Half the participants received a message meant to feel less confrontational, inviting them to reflect on how Black people face unequal treatment in society, and to consider being fairer in the judgments they passed. The other half of the participants received a message that was more confrontational: It told them that their responses made them "sound like some kind of racist" and said they should think about Black people in less prejudiced ways.

It's easy to understand how being called "racist" by a stranger after a brief virtual interaction would feel confrontational—and even threatening. And indeed, participants were more likely to agree that the second message felt like a personal attack. (In contrast, participants were more likely to agree that the *less* confrontational language was a "casual, nonthreatening suggestion.") And yet, regardless of the type of language used (confrontational or suggestive), *all* participants reported feeling a similar degree of negative self-directed affect—that feeling of emotional discomfort stemming from one's own perceived shortcomings or missteps. In other words, study participants felt angry at and disappointed in themselves, guilty, and regretful for holding biased views. Most significantly, when they were given a chance to redo the inference task, all participants showed a marked decrease in stereotypical responding.

The feelings elicited when we're forced to confront our own bias are uncomfortable, but they're also essential. They spark the reflection needed for meaningful change—a signal that the process of reducing bias is already in motion. And this particular study seemed to indicate that these emotions would surface no matter how a person was confronted, prompting at least a temporary shift in awareness and behavior.

As my understanding of the power of confronting bias grew, I began conducting workshops to teach others about the insights I'd gathered. Each time I reiterated that saying anything was better than staying silent—and supported it with research—I could visibly see the relief on my audience's faces. Time and again, participants recalled situations in which they could have spoken up against bias but didn't, and were left grappling with the guilt of not having known how to intervene. Like me in my Facebook encounter, they'd put so much pressure on themselves to say the perfect thing. The idea that they didn't need to be flawless—they just needed to be vocal—was freeing.

Yet, the more I spoke with attendees at my Confronting Bias workshops, the more I came to realize that my "just say anything" guidance was incomplete. I'd been presenting confronting bias as a simple three-step process: (1) say something (anything!), (2) let the negative self-directed emotions that arise do the heavy lifting, and (3) presto-chango, the biased behavior is banished. And it was true that the research lent credence to this seemingly straightforward path. But while research studies are useful, inquiries conducted in a lab fall short of capturing the complex dynamics of real-world human interaction. For one, these experiments typically transpire over the course of a thirty-to-sixty-minute time frame, while our real-world relationships unfold over a much longer period than that. Moreover, research environments are carefully controlled—participants intentionally have limited choices so that researchers can easily make comparisons—but in real life our choices are never as binary or clear-cut as research suggests. It was clear that confronting bias *did* often change behavior, but it was a mistake to present the process as simplistically as I'd been doing. As I reflected on the research with this new perspective, I realized I needed to revise the way I framed my own Facebook experience with Tracy.

Confronting bias is rarely simple, and my encounter with Tracy is strong proof of that fact. Even now, ten years later, when I think back on that interaction, I remember nearly everything about the moments *before* I decided to respond to her post: the frustration that I felt at realizing that someone in my close circle was so homophobic; the pit in my stomach that refused to go away until I found the courage to take action; and the relief that flooded in after I posted my comment on her page. But after that? I've got nothing. I don't remember if I ever went back to her post to see if she—or anyone else for that matter—responded to what I'd written. In fact, I don't recall having any further conversation with her on the topic at all. What I do know is that Tracy and I are no longer friends. There are a multitude of reasons why this is so, but it's likely that our Facebook conflict created, or exacerbated, that fracture. Perhaps that disagreement signaled to one or both of us that we weren't compatible and our friendship wasn't worth saving.

The even more unfortunate piece is that, because our subsequent interactions are nonexistent and/or lost in my memory, I don't even know whether my carefully crafted confrontation actually *changed* anything. I wish I could add in a footnote here about how our interaction profoundly impacted Tracy, or how I've witnessed her attitude toward gay people evolve in the years since. But as much as I hope this is the case, it's entirely possible that our exchange was barely a blip on her radar. There's no proverbial bow with which I can tie up my story; in *this* instance, I have no anecdotal evidence that confronting bias worked.

Even so, there were other wins to celebrate. For one, while this first attempt at confronting bias was clunky, the practice I gained in that situation helped me tremendously in future ones. And, while this relationship didn't stand the test of time, I have other examples—both from my own experiences and from those of people I've interviewed in my research— of relationships that not only endured bias confrontation but grew stronger because of it. So while we can never predict exactly how someone will respond in a given situation, there's good reason to believe that when you show someone you value them enough to hold them accountable, they're more likely to listen—and the relationship between you may deepen in the process. As humans, our role is simply to do our best, learn from each experience, and evolve along the way.

My experience with Tracy, and the stories I heard from my workshop attendees and research participants, affirmed that confronting bias can be challenging for myriad reasons.[9] I heard stories from people who were devastated because calling out bias hadn't altered the other person's behavior—but it *had* strained, or even broken, a close relationship. I fielded questions from people about calling out bias where there were power dynamics at play, or in echo chambers where dissent was unwelcome. I spoke to people weighing the very real fear that speaking up might put them in harm's way. As much as I remained confident that the benefits of confronting bias outweighed the risks—the societal norms of inclusion and equity are foundational to our ability to coexist—I knew that I had to help people understand how to navigate the potentially tricky terrain ahead.

As I reflected on how to better integrate my research-based insights with the realities of human interaction, I updated my workshop materials and fine-tuned my signature tagline about confronting bias. First, I reminded people about the importance of calling out bias and reinforcing inclusive norms. I spoke about the harm that bias does, both to the individual(s) targeted by the comments or behavior and to our society. I spoke about how there were some situations that simply called for strong language, and that if people were *solely* interested in stopping the harm, they could say anything. However, I also acknowledged that most people were witnessing biased behavior of their friends, colleagues, and loved ones. In those instances, we generally have two goals: We want the person to change their behavior—in both the short term and the long term—and we also want to preserve (and, ideally, deepen) the relationship. Let's be clear: Saying anything is always better than saying nothing at all. But if you want to create the best possible outcome, there is a gold standard when it comes to confronting bias that not only alters behavior in the short term but also preserves relationships and supports lasting behavioral shifts. This approach relies on two core beliefs—one we've already discussed in another context, and one we haven't.

CALLING OUT BIAS WITH CARE HAS AN EVEN GREATER IMPACT

In chapter 1, we explored how adopting a growth mindset helps us identify and unlearn our own biases. But this belief—that bias isn't fixed and that overcoming it is a skill—can also transform how we engage with others, fostering more productive and compassionate interactions.

Confronting bias with the belief that people can grow helps them see that potential in themselves. When you offer feedback for future improvement, you're demonstrating faith in their ability to change. Moreover, when the confronter adopts growth-mindset language, they mitigate unpleasant reactions such as defensiveness, lashing out, or shutting down. For example, in one study, researchers again used the paradigm in which participants were asked to infer individuals' occupations.[10] When those participants made the predictable biased inferences, some of them received feedback using growth-mindset language: "I know this task was a little weird, but I thought some of your answers on the photos of Black people were a little prejudiced, and that bothered me...I wanted to point it out because I think people can work on these things and change how biased they are." These participants responded much more positively than those who received a fixed-mindset message, which began the same way, but ended with "I wanted to point it out, but I don't think people can do much to change how biased they are." This second group responded far less favorably, highlighting the impact of framing bias as something that can be improved rather than an unchangeable trait.[11] Furthermore, participants who received the growth-mindset message evaluated their confronters more positively after the interaction— perceiving them as friendlier, more personable, warmer, and more approachable than participants who received the fixed-mindset confrontation. Of course, no one sentence can magically resolve all interpersonal conflict. But it *is* helpful to know that affirming someone's capacity to do better can help disarm some of the challenges that might otherwise arise.

Another reason that confronting bias can be interpersonally risky is that nobody likes to feel ignorant or uninformed— yet that's often the unintended effect of calling it out. Many of us have likely muttered to ourselves about how someone who makes a racist comment must be an uneducated idiot—much like I did when I criticized Tracy's character to my partner. Even if we're not calling the person racist *outright*, language that is condescending or chastising is still threatening in its own way, and attacks on a person's character rarely communicate a belief in their ability to grow or change. For example, saying to someone who's a generation or more your senior, "I know there was less emphasis on political correctness when you were growing up, but things are different now," suggests not only that they don't know any better but that they can *never* know, or do, better because their biases are inextricably linked to the era in which they grew up. The inherent moral superiority in such a statement triggers a defensive response, and while the research shows that their behavior may change for the better anyway, this kind of language does little to entice someone to listen to anything we have to say next.[12] Expressing confidence in someone's ability to change can mitigate these feelings. Explicitly appealing to their autonomy enhances the impact.

When persuading people to adjust their behavior, messages that emphasize their agency to determine their own outcomes in life are more likely to lead to long-lasting behavior change than messages suggesting their choices have little impact on their outcomes. This concept has been applied to a broad range of behaviors, including smoking cessation, exercise and weight loss, and educational attainment.[13] In all cases, a framing that encourages people to adopt new behaviors by emphasizing their autonomy, their competence, and their interconnectedness to others leads to greater behavior adoption.

The same considerations are relevant when addressing racial bias. In one study, researchers told college student participants they were testing out a new campus initiative to reduce prejudice.[14] One group of students received a brochure underscoring how nonprejudiced behavior contributes to a more equitable society and enhances individual happiness and deeper engagement with the world. It then reminded participants that they had a choice in the matter: "You are free to choose to value nonprejudice. Only <u>you</u> can decide to be an egalitarian person." Another group received brochures that were much more authoritarian in their language. Students "must" control their prejudice, they were told, in order to be good citizens and avoid "serious consequences" like losing their jobs or social exile. The final sentences stripped away any illusion of choice: "In today's multicultural society, we should all be less prejudiced. We should all refrain from negative stereotyping. It is, after all, the politically and socially correct thing to do, and it's something that society demands of us." A third group of participants, who served as the control group, received a brochure that included a definition of prejudice but no further information on reasons for reducing one's prejudice.

The first brochure, which emphasized autonomy, proved significantly more effective in multiple ways. Participants who received *this* brochure reported a greater intrinsic desire to be nonprejudiced (e.g., agreeing that avoiding prejudice was important because "tolerance is important to me"), reported less anti-Black bias, and showed no implicit preference for White people over Black people compared to participants who read the controlling message.

You're likely not handing out brochures to your friends and family stressing the importance of reducing racial bias, but these insights provide an effective blueprint for the kind of language you could use to call out bias in everyday settings. To appeal to someone's sense of autonomy, use wording that emphasizes their power to think differently: "Have you considered a different perspective?" or "That's one way to look at it, but you might think about it this other way, too." To affirm that you view them as competent individuals capable of change, frame the discussion as if there's more to the topic than they (yet) know. The problem is *not* that they're stupid (which is a limiting, fixed-mindset label); it's that they haven't been exposed to information that could shape their thinking. Phrases like "I read an article on this topic that you might enjoy" or "Could I share something I learned that helped influence my thinking on this?" signal that you believe they might reconsider their perspective with the benefit of exposure to new ideas. Finally, remember that humans are social beings. No one wants to feel as though they're alone on an amoral island. Pointing out their isolated viewpoint—"Wow, I haven't heard someone say *that* in forever"—will only intensify any feelings of exclusion they might already be experiencing. (Besides, the reality is that their perspective might not be much different from your own previous thinking—the growth-mindset emphasis on gradual change is helpful in this context.) Tapping into shared values with statements like "I know we both genuinely care about the impact our actions have on others, which is why I wanted to talk to you about this," is one way to forefront this interconnectedness. Another approach is to be vulnerable and share some of your own journey: "I used to make remarks like that, too, and I didn't realize their impact. But over time—and thanks to supportive friends who've given me some honest reflections—I've changed my perspective." Use these words as a foundation, adapt them to your style, and then practice, practice, practice.[15] Preparation is a great way to ensure the behavior you *believe* you'd exhibit in a hypothetical situation is the behavior you *actually* exhibit in the moment.

PUBLIC DECLARATIONS: MEANINGFUL ACTION OR MEANINGLESS VIRTUE SIGNALING?

One-on-one dialogues offer a space where bias can be directly confronted, but opportunities to confront bias and/or emphasize antibias values happen at scale, too. In June 2016, 52 percent of British voters shocked the world by voting in favor of the UK's withdrawal from the European Union. Brexit was seen by many as the latest in a wave of xenophobic policies gaining traction worldwide—one that left opponents of the "leave" vote wondering how they could signal that they believed their country was, and should remain, a welcome place for immigrants and ethnic minority communities. In a time of national unrest, one woman proposed using safety pins as a subtle way to signal support for immigrant and ethnic minority communities in the UK.[16] (Months later, in the aftermath of Donald Trump's election win, safety pins emerged as a symbol of support for victims of racist, religious, or homophobic abuse in the United States.) Her intention was that the safety pin be understood as more than a symbol; she wanted it to demonstrate the wearer's commitment to confronting racist behavior. The idea was that, at a time when it was difficult to gauge someone's stance on the issue (after all, the country had been split almost fifty-fifty), this overt expression of values would be reassuring for those feeling especially vulnerable.

The safety pin was certainly not the first time this kind of symbol had been adopted by a mass protest movement, but it did seem to usher in a host of new ways for people to profess their values.[17] Around the world, university students and corporate employees began to adorn their laptops and social media profiles with badges, stickers, or other tokens they had received in exchange for completing programs on how to be an effective ally to military veterans, the LGBTQ+ community, religious minorities, and others. In the digital world, activism could be distilled to symbols, and signaling your values could be "done" in a few clicks—updating your email signature with pronouns, adding #StopAsianHate to your Twitter bio, posting a black square on Instagram, or decorating your profile with a Ukrainian flag, a watermelon, a Pride flag, and so on.[18] Critics mocked these gestures as examples of "performative allyship" or "slacktivism," contending that they were more about distancing oneself from the "bad people" on the other side of the issue than they were about genuine solidarity with marginalized communities.[19] In the case of the safety pin, critics questioned where those expressing outrage at Brexit had been in the days, months, and years leading up to it. After all, the Brexit referendum vote didn't materialize suddenly; it was the result of people tolerating years of anti-immigrant comments from friends, family, and colleagues, which fueled a nationwide campaign of hate. Similarly, those donning "Not My President" merchandise were confronted with the reality that Trump's rise to power didn't happen in isolation; it was enabled by years of silence from those who could've challenged the growing tide of xenophobia, Islamophobia, and ableism in the United States but chose not to speak up. To don a safety pin or a slogan to express your disdain after the fact—when your inaction may have contributed to the very outcome you now decry—is not solidarity at all, the critics asserted.

There are three things that trouble me about this critique. The first is that I personally believe that these symbolic protests *can* open the door for an ongoing conversation about bias, among other social ills. In fact, this has been my experience. For example, when I was in college, it was common for people to change their Facebook profile pictures to signal their stances on various issues. Marriage equality in the United States was a prominent debate at the time, and I changed my profile picture to the logo for the Human Rights Campaign to show my support for gay marriage. A family member noticed the change and sent me a private message: "What's that a picture of?" I explained that it was my way of showing support for gay marriage, and we had a brief conversation about why I felt it was so important to publicly declare that belief. The fact that this particular family member even responded was a victory of its own kind—this was someone who'd previously said that they would "tolerate" gay people but wouldn't accept their "lifestyle." So it felt like a major win to be able to broach a conversation about LGBTQ+ rights with them in this relatively low-stakes way.

Moreover, these symbolic protests can highlight the prevailing public sentiment on an issue. For example, a White person who feels inconvenienced by a racial justice protest that disrupts their commute to work may later observe that many of their close (White) friends have #BlackLivesMatter posts on their social media accounts, prompting them to recognize that their perspective is not widely shared. Wanting to understand more or to preserve their friendships, they may engage in conversations that gradually reshape their views. This is how, at their best, public declarations of values can send a powerful message to others about what one believes, and apply a bit of positive peer pressure that encourages others to follow suit.

My second issue with dismissing symbolic gestures as mere virtue signaling is that it assumes a fixed mindset—ignoring the fact that behaviors and beliefs can evolve with new experiences and insights. For example, maybe someone wearing a safety pin *is* just doing so because it's fashionable, and not something they'd have chosen to do independently. But maybe this person was *also* shocked by the outcome of the Brexit vote and suddenly realizes they've been far too silent until now—that they should hold themselves accountable (and be held accountable) for the role they played in that outcome. The theory of planned behavior suggests that people are much more likely to follow through on an action when they first demonstrate a plan to engage in that action.[20] Perhaps the safety pin demonstrates the person's intent to be more egalitarian, thereby encouraging them to behave in a way that's consistent with those values. Viewed through *this* lens, the safety pin becomes their first foray into sincere behavior change and accountability.

And what if wearing that pin opens the door to conversations they wouldn't have had otherwise, leading to invitations to teach-ins and protests they might never have discovered? What if, a year later, they're no longer donning that safety pin (and perhaps feel a little embarrassed that they ever did so) because they now know about far more effective ways to combat anti-immigrant policies and sentiments?[21] *This* possibility is why I spend less time hand-wringing over whether a person's current behavior is performative, and instead look at the entire trajectory of their actions—past, present, and future. That's where the most meaningful insights about someone's journey emerge.

Finally, critiques about symbolic protests often overlook the fact that public displays can be safety cues for people from marginalized backgrounds. For example, as new homeowners, my husband and I would walk around our neighborhood and take note of the houses that had yard signs with statements like "In this house we believe..." (followed by a litany of progressive beliefs). Apprehensive about being one of the few young Black couples—if not the only one—in the neighborhood, we were reassured by those signs that our neighbors likely shared our values, and this affirmed that we'd chosen the right place to raise our family.

A student undergoing a gender transition may feel both relieved and reassured to see a Pride flag sticker on their professor's office door alongside the words "You Are Welcome Here"—it demonstrates that the professor likely won't balk at the student's request to change their name and pronouns midsemester. An employee may be reticent to ask their manager for a day off to observe their cultural or religious holiday until they see the badge on the person's Slack profile indicating completion of the company's inclusion trainings (the content of which often includes recognizing the many important dates that don't fall on the "conventional" calendar). The person who is grieving an eruption of violence against others who share their identity may feel less pressure to paste on a smile and offer a rote response when a coworker asks, "How are you doing?" if they know that person recently shared something on social media expressing sympathy for the victims of that violence. That post signals that their peer may be more prepared to handle a genuine, unfiltered answer. People who are underrepresented in *any* setting will always wonder whether they are welcome, valued, and supported; symbolic manifestations of their peers' and leaders' beliefs—so long as they're backed up with actions that *uphold* those beliefs—can alleviate some of that uncertainty.

About a year after George Floyd's murder, I got a tattoo on my left forearm of roses in various stages of development.

From the delicate baby buds (my favorite), to the closed bulbs eager to blossom, to the roses in full bloom, these flowers were a reminder that growth is often gradual, unfolding at its own pace. Over the preceding year, I'd spoken to countless people who were disheartened by the lack of meaningful change following the United States' "summer of racial reckoning." But, ever the optimist, I still believed that positive change was on the horizon. I believed—and still do—that confronting bias was like planting a garden: One needed to prepare the soil to ensure the seed would take, plant the seed, water the flower bed, prune away the weeds that threaten the nascent bloom's growth, and so on. I reminded others (and myself) that we were embarking on a community effort to plant a garden and that we all had a vital role to play. Some days, as I challenged deeply held racist mindsets, it felt very much like I was at the early, thankless stage of tilling soil to ensure the seeds planted later would find fertile ground. Other days, I was deep in the mud as I watered the dirt, helping to nurture the seeds of anti-racism that had already been planted. And there were *also* the days when I witnessed the joy of a flower blooming, as someone not only embraced a new perspective but also shared a transformative conversation they'd had with a friend, colleague, or family member. This analogy underscores why we *all* must take responsibility for confronting bias. You may not know where someone is on their growth journey, but if you miss your opportunity to till the soil, water the dirt, or prune the weeds where you meet them, you're failing to contribute to the collective effort to change attitudes and behavior for the better.

This is not to downplay how difficult confronting bias can be. In a garden, it's not always obvious which seeds have already been sown, or which plants need extra care versus those that can thrive independently for now. And sometimes, we just don't have the luxury of time. A garden can take months or even years to cultivate, and when people's rights and lives are on the line, we need change immediately. In moments like this, I look for fertile soil: the places where we have the greatest opportunity to effect change, where time works in our favor, and where we can see the rewards of our efforts unfold.

When it comes to social change, I believe that children are our most fertile ground. Addressing bias in adults involves challenging established beliefs, deconstructing outdated mindsets, and offering reeducation. *Children's* minds, however, are receptive to new ideas precisely because they don't require unlearning old patterns first; instead, we can introduce them to inclusive values, norms, and ideas from the start. If we are to build the bias-free world we envision, we need to nurture children who *instinctively* embrace equity and reject bias.

CHAPTER 8

Equipping Children to Detect and Challenge Racial Bias

From as far back as I can remember, I've loved children. Long before I became a parent, I naturally gravitated toward caregiving roles—from babysitting through my teenage years, to eagerly embracing the role of active and doting auntie the moment my niece entered the world, to enthusiastically volunteering to care for a friend's child so they could go to a movie or take a nap. Children are brimming with promise and wonder, and their presence never fails to refresh my own perspective on life. When accompanied by a toddler, something as ordinary as a walk is transformed into an extraordinary adventure as they marvel at each new discovery: We extend our arms wide whenever a plane or bird soars above us to pretend *we're* flying, too; and as we squat on the pavement, we marvel at the ants' orderly march, then practice our own version of their disciplined formation— the toddler in the lead. If I were walking alone, my adult instincts might be to complain about the noise pollution from the plane or trample the ants beneath my feet. But spending time with children, and seeing the world through their eyes, allows me to slow down and rediscover the enchantment in everyday life.

Perhaps it's because children represent a pure *potential* for good that adults look to them as evidence that the world will be in better hands when they're at the helm. We look at them as sources of boundless possibility and imagine the future they might shape: Will they discover a cure for cancer? Will they find a way to permanently enshrine women's rights or reverse climate change? Will they be the ones to disman-tle racism, homophobia, and society's other injustices? We convince ourselves that the younger generations—who are more racially diverse than their predecessors and thus pre-sumably more progressive on issues of race and identity—will be better equipped to resolve the world's inequities and will be effective where we *couldn't* be.

Every generation has had their own version of this narra-tive, with each new wave of youth being heralded as the most enlightened, progressive, and well-informed yet.[1] But inev-itably, as their youth wanes and the glow of their potential diminishes, less flattering data begins to surface, revealing how this once-young generation is beginning to mirror the older adults they once seemed so refreshingly divergent from.[2] Take baby boomers, for instance, whose fervent protests against the Vietnam War and radical embrace of alternative lifestyles—including their free-spirited attitudes toward drugs and sex—were immortalized by the Summer of Love. The once-radical, countercultural spirit that defined the baby boomer generation has shifted over time, giving way to phrases like "Okay, boomer"—younger generations' shorthand for boomers' perceived disconnect from modern realities. Their radical identity long forgotten, boomers are now often seen as the most conservative generation in the United States, with younger cohorts viewing them as out of touch with today's social and political landscape.[3]

As a Millennial, I've experienced my own generation's version of this evolution firsthand. I remember quite vividly how many people marveled at my generation's counterculture habits: the renaissance of student activism, a push for more socially conscious consumption, and our own pro-drug stances to boot. The young Millennials who came of age post-9/11 were disillusioned with the state of the world, more radical than their parents, and unafraid to take their concerns to the streets. Our more progressive views were reflected in the policies we supported, the brands we chose, and the president we elected in 2008 and 2012.[4] Over time, however, the narrative of Millennials as boundary pushers who would buck the trends of previous generations faded. In their place came new polls and new headlines, indicating that Millennials weren't so different from previous generations after all.

In 2015, a team at the *Washington Post* reviewed data on five measures of racial prejudice collected through the General Social Survey by NORC (previously the National Opinion Research Center) and compared the results across generations. The headline said everything there was to know about the findings: "Millennials Are Just as Racist as Their Parents."[5] On nearly every single indicator, White Millennials' attitudes about Black people aligned closely with those of Gen X and baby boomers. For example, 31 percent of Millennials rated Black people as lazier / less hardworking than White people, a view shared by 32 percent of Gen X and 35 percent of baby boomer respondents. Similar percentages of Millennials and baby boomers (23 percent and 24 percent, respectively) rated Black people as less intelligent than White people. Although there were *some* meaningful differences in Millennials' attitudes when compared to those of their Silent Generation grandparents (perhaps Millennials are just as racist as their parents, but not *quite* as racist as their grandparents), the findings largely contradicted the perception that Millennials were a "post-racial" generation.

In the years that followed, further research underscored the persistence of racial bias across generations. In one study, researchers responded to more than four thousand "roommate wanted" ads placed in US metropolitan areas, varying the names of the applicants in ways intended to indicate the race of the ostensible roommate.[6] Housing audit studies like these have been conducted since the 1970s, and the results typically highlight the discrimination that people of color face relative to White people. This 2020 study was no different: Potential roommates with names that sounded White were far more likely to get responses than those with names that suggested Asian, Black, or Hispanic heritage, further shattering the image of "the woke Millennial."

We're currently witnessing a similar shift with Gen Z, who were most recently celebrated as the anti-racist beacons of the future because of their multiracial identities, awareness of racism, and embrace of gender fluidity and non-binary pronouns.[7] Today's headlines are beginning to tell a different story: "Gen Z Isn't as Anti-Racist as You Think,"[8] one cautions, while another draws attention to the fact that Gen Z's ostensible progressivism did *not* bear out in the 2024 presidential election, when 56 percent of men between the ages of eighteen and twenty-nine voted for Donald Trump.[9] The evidence is clear: While generational shifts may bring changes in perspectives, no single generation can completely transcend the ingrained biases and challenges of previous ones.

So why does this misconception endure? I believe it's because most people like to think that racial progress happens organically rather than intentionally. People seem willing to behave as though our society exists on some conveyor belt of chronological time that will necessarily deliver us to a more equitable future—regardless of whether we actually *do* anything to bring about this evolution. In *this* worldview, racism will diminish on its own with each passing generation, simply as a product of time.

This misguided vision of change heavily underestimates (among other things) the role that we play in shaping the racial views and convictions of whatever generation is coming of age. And if each new generation inherits their beliefs largely from their parents, can we expect children raised by biased parents to be anything but biased? The answer is that it depends—on whether those parents accept responsibility for the intentional work of rearing children who critically question what they've been taught (or what's been modeled for them), reflect on the world around them, and choose a perspective rooted in equity rather than bias.

As the first curators of our children's experiences, we must take seriously the fact that children will repeat the biases and behaviors they observe in the influential adults in their lives. That means if we engage in conversations about racism and actively work to dismantle it, there's a very strong likelihood our children will follow suit. But it *also* means that if we stay silent on the topic, our children will mirror our example. And, finally, it means that if we are perpetuating racism, we should not be surprised when our children do too. This is why parents *must* be proactive in nurturing children who can identify and confront bias to pave the way to a more equitable world.

HOW DO WHITE CHILDREN LEARN ABOUT
RACE AND RACISM?

Years ago, I was sitting in a waiting room and riffling through the magazines that peppered the tables in the area. One of them immediately caught my attention. The cover featured the face of an adorable White baby, its large dark gray eyes gazing up at me inquisitively. Accompanying the photo was a single question, written in black block letters across the baby's forehead: "IS YOUR BABY RACIST?" The cover of this September 2009 issue of *Newsweek* was clearly designed to stop people in their tracks and compel them to pick up the magazine (in that respect, I played right into the editor's hands!), but the cover story broached an important question: How and when *do* young children learn about race and racism?

Clickbait headlines notwithstanding, how children's racial perceptions develop is a very valid inquiry.[10] Babies certainly aren't born with the prevailing societal stereotypes and racist beliefs preprogrammed into their brains—but they also don't remain blank slates for very long. Evidence suggests that even the youngest of infants use racial cues to some degree in their decision-making. For example, infants as young as three months old show a preference for faces that resemble the ones they see most often (usually those of their own race).[11] At this stage, the preference seems to be driven more by pattern recognition and instinct than by any awareness of race:

Babies are closely attuned to the people who keep them safe, happy, and fed, so they may be comforted by faces that look like those who consistently provide for them. The problem is that, without intervention, what begins as a simple preference for familiarity can eventually transform into preferences that reflect the biases and prejudices present in the culture.

To illustrate how this can happen, here's a story about the first time I distinctly recall being on the receiving end of racism: I was about four years old, and one of my friends at school, Tanner, had brought in a stamp pad and a new set of rubber stamps to show off.[12] A few of us were huddled around the cubbies waiting for Tanner to open his backpack to reveal his small treasure. When he finally did, we all appreciatively oohed and aahed, clamoring for a closer look. When Tanner indicated that he meant to share his bounty with the group, everyone—myself included—stuck out their hand to receive a stamp. Within moments, my excitement turned to crushing disappointment as Tanner gave every one of our friends a stamp but refused to give one to me. He explained his decision very matter-of-factly: The ink wouldn't show up on my skin, so there was no point. I tried to act indifferent on the outside, but inside, I was devastated.

As I've reflected on this formative experience over the years, I find myself less interested in defining Tanner's actions as racist (remember, we're talking about a four-year-old here), and more curious about the influences that shaped his behavior that day. One major factor at play was certainly

Tanner's social context. Most White children grow up in mostly White or entirely White environments—indeed, I was one of the few non-White children in my class, and likely one of the few non-White people that Tanner interacted with anywhere in his life—so his exposure to people from other races was probably quite limited. And this exposure is critical, especially during a child's earliest and most formative years. Studies indicate that by preschool age, children from dominant social groups (e.g., White children) tend to exhibit a strong preference for their own group, associating it with positive traits and viewing other racial groups more negatively.[13] This looks markedly different among children of color, who show only a modest in-group preference and *also* show a preference for White people over those from other racial minority groups.[14] The simplest reason for this is that children of color learn quite early about their society's racial hierarchy—often through experiences like the one I had with Tanner. These early experiences make it challenging to maintain a robust preference for their own group in the face of repeated messages that their group is not valued.

The in-group favoritism that White children exhibit is especially pronounced among White children who are raised in racially homogeneous environments. But limited exposure to people of color isn't the only culprit. The more difficult truth to swallow is that children learn bias from the patterns they observe and internalize in their environment. It's doubtful that Tanner's parents directly instructed him not to share his stamps with Black children; instead, Tanner probably learned that sharing with Black children was unimportant through indirect yet powerful signals.

There's ample evidence indicating that children are particularly adept at picking up on subtle behaviors and patterns from a young age, even if they don't have the language to articulate what they're seeing. Like budding scientists, children assess the social world by observing the people and behaviors around them, piecing together their ideas about race and racism through these interactions. Perhaps, during playtime at the park, Tanner noticed that his parents were insistent that he share his toys with the other White children but were *less* insistent about enforcing "the sharing rule" with non-White children. Perhaps he observed his parents smiling at the other White people they passed on the street but averting their gaze when a Black family approached. From there, Tanner may have noticed patterns that emerged in a variety of contexts. Maybe it's not just that his *parents* were more lax about his sharing with non-White children but that his *teacher* didn't really police his sharing with those children either. Maybe it's not just that Tanner's teacher always seemed to have a shorter temper with his Black classmate, but it's also that he witnessed his aunt's impatience when she placed an order with a Black restaurant server. Tanner's parents, family members, and teacher may have been utterly oblivious to the messages they were sending in these fleeting moments, but these experiences would nonetheless have marked Tanner's early exposure to racism.

Research shows that children are more likely to be influenced by the behaviors they witness from the adults in their lives than they are by the words those adults speak. In a study of approximately one hundred White families with children between the ages of five and seven, researchers discovered that the strongest predictor of a child's racial attitudes was what the children *perceived* their parents' attitudes to be.[15] For example, whereas most parents in the study reported having Black friends (69 percent of mothers and 78 percent of fathers), only 53 percent of their children were aware of those interracial friendships. And it was the *awareness* of the friendships that mattered: Children who knew their parents had Black friends held significantly more positive views of Black people than those whose parents had no Black friends, or who were unaware of any such friendships. In other words, your child's perceptions of race may be less impacted by your verbal claims that all people are equally good and wonderful. Instead, they're watching how you interact with others, picking up on subtle cues about whom you respect, trust, or avoid. They're using *those* clues to determine what you really believe—and, in turn, what *they* should believe, too.

While actions often speak louder than words, words matter a lot, too: Extant research demonstrates that one reason White children learn about race, racial identity, and racism much later than children of color do is because, in many cases, their parents aren't initiating open, honest conversations about race.[16] And even those parents who *do* are often uninformed about just how early and frequent those intentional anti-racist interventions need to be. Even though children as young as three are capable of understanding—and mimicking—the racist patterns of their society (assigning more desirable traits to White people, for example), parents underestimate the age at which children have the capacity for race-related conversations by about four and a half years.[17] Moreover, fear about how to broach these sensitive conversations with children keeps adults silent in the key teachable moments when they *should* be active participants in shaping their children's views.

Research shows that having race-related conversations can help parents clarify their own beliefs and perspectives about race for their children. For example, in that study examining the relationship between the racial attitudes of White parents and children, half of the White children participating initially had no idea whether their parents had positive views about Black people. But after their parents engaged them in conversations about race (and/or exposed them to educational videos featuring diverse characters and positive portrayals of cross-racial friendships), only 19 percent remained uncertain of their parents' racial beliefs.

The message is clear: By leaving children to draw their own conclusions about race and racism, White parents are all but guaranteeing their children will develop and act upon the same racial biases already present in the world. However, those who take intentional, proactive steps to raise children who can identify and fight racial bias using the kinds of strategies described in this chapter will find their efforts pay off considerably.

TEACH (AND MODEL) COLOR CONSCIOUSNESS

The situation with Tanner unfolded in a setting where no adults were observing, but let's imagine for a moment that our interaction happened with his parents as witnesses. Should they have chosen to address his behavior with him, they might have taken one of two approaches. The first—an approach much more common among White parents—would involve adopting a color-blind stance, telling Tanner that my darker skin doesn't make me any different from him. The flaw in this response is that it's quite evidently false—*anyone*, Tanner included, can see that we *are* different. Moreover, the reality is that a light blue stamp *wouldn't* show up on my skin as it would on my classmates'. Pretending otherwise wouldn't erase the difference; it would simply create a different kind of alienation—one that denies my reality rather than acknowledging it.

What if, instead, Tanner's parents took an approach that acknowledged my darker skin *and* encouraged him to treat me the same way he treated our other friends? They might say, "Just because Evelyn has darker skin doesn't mean she doesn't want a stamp. It's not very nice to leave someone out because they are different from us. Let's find a way to share with Evelyn, too." This color-conscious approach could open other doors of possibility. After all, kids are incredibly creative problem-solvers! In the color-conscious version of this scenario, I can imagine a young Tanner scanning the other colors on his stamp palette and choosing one that would be just as vibrant on my darker skin. *This* is the difference between color blindness and color consciousness: Whereas the first approach overlooks our differences, the second recognizes them and adapts accordingly.

The folly of teaching children color blindness lies in the fact that children are biologically hardwired to perceive differences. From their earliest days of infancy, we teach children how to categorize objects by color, size, shape, and the like. By the time they're three years old, children have learned to apply that same logic to people, as they come to learn that there are a multitude of ways that people can look. This is the natural progression of human development, but parents frequently express concern when their children start observing and acknowledging the differences among people—including skin tone, and then race. Like that *Newsweek* cover story, they fear it's a sign that their baby is racist. But awareness of racial differences is not the same as racism (even if it *is* true that the window of innocence between observing racial differences and exhibiting racist behaviors is quite small).[18] And as we've seen, teaching color blindness doesn't prevent racism—in fact, it risks perpetuating it. Adults must break free from color-blind thinking and instill in their children the importance of accepting and honoring people's differences.

The opportunities to do this are likely all around you. I remember vividly the evening when my then three-year-old niece sidled up next to me, aligning her forearm next to mine as she proudly declared, "Auntie RAE, my skin is darker than yours." The assertion seemed to come from out of nowhere, but I knew that she was doing what three-year-olds do best—noticing things—so I embraced the opening she gave me and continued the conversation: "It *is*! What made you notice that?" She went on to share that her teacher had darker skin than she did, and all her friends at school had different skin tones, too—some of them were lighter than hers. I inquired further: "Oh really? Cool! What else do you notice about your friends?" I learned that day that some of her friends had curly hair and some had straight hair, some had blue eyes and others had brown eyes. She also shared details about their interests, like who enjoyed playing with trains or coloring. This is a powerful way for parents to teach and model color consciousness: Rather than shutting down conversations about differences—racial or otherwise—embrace children's curiosity and invite them to share what they observe! By doing so, you reinforce that differences are not only okay but worth understanding, laying a foundation for deeper awareness that will evolve as they grow. (You also nurture their natural curiosity—a crucial trait for developing a growth mindset and a lifelong willingness to learn.)

USE DIVERSE MEDIA TO EXPOSE CHILDREN
TO NEW IDEAS AND PEOPLE

Teaching and modeling color consciousness are great ways to foster children's awareness about race. But in order to practice acknowledging and celebrating diversity, children need access to environments that are racially diverse. Remember that children's preferences for race are shaped by the exposure they receive. Use this insight to actively introduce them to diverse cultures, identities, and experiences, in both direct and indirect ways.

One of my favorite suggestions for parents is to take a close look at the books on their children's shelves. To give you some sense of what this could look like, I'll share my approach for my daughter's library. Because she is a young Black girl, I want her to read stories that feature Black people *and* people of other races and skin tones in empowering positions like leaders and heroes. I want her to be aware of her history as an African American and a descendant of slavery, while also underscoring that our people's connection to slavery is hardly the only noteworthy thing about us. I also want my daughter to understand that families come in many different forms: Her friends may be raised by two parents of the same gender, by a single parent, by grandparents or other family members, or by any other combination of possibilities. While our neighborhood is fairly diverse, I recognize that our circle of friends doesn't fully reflect the variety of identities, beliefs, and customs out there. I want my daughter's instinct to be curiosity and acceptance, *not* disdain and rejection, when she encounters people who are different from her, so I select stories that help fill in those gaps. I also gravitate toward books that reinforce values that are important to our family, like caring for others and standing up for what you believe in.

This kind of curation requires more than a surface-level inspection of a book's cover and a cursory skim of its pages. I read the book carefully to make sure the core message is one of inclusion, and I'm not afraid to veto a book if it doesn't pass muster. (If you're thinking to yourself that this is a tall order for a child's library, you may be right—but in the same way that raising kids to be healthy and strong requires paying attention to the foods they're consuming, raising kids to detect bias requires paying attention to the messages in the *stories* they're consuming as well.) Not *every* book will meet *all* these criteria, but having these goals in mind has helped me curate a richly diverse range of stories.

You can use a similar framework when building your children's libraries. The first step is being intentional about building diverse representation in those stories—something that will undoubtedly take effort. In fact, your child's books are more likely to feature animals or objects (e.g., monsters, trucks) as main characters than they are people of color: 38 percent of children's books published in the UK in 2019 included the former, while just 5 percent of books published in the same time frame included the latter.[19] Moreover, a 2021 study done in the US found that 44 percent of children's books *solely* feature White characters.[20] Of course, there's nothing wrong with having White characters in your child's books—but if they're the *only* characters your children encounter, you'll be reinforcing the belief that White people are the default in society, and the only people worth knowing about.

If you're uncertain about how to begin, take inventory of your social circle to see which groups are underrepresented and where your child might benefit from more exposure. Sometimes this can be as simple as opting for a story featuring a non-White protagonist. For example, Don Freeman's *Corduroy* is a story about a little Black girl who loves a stuffed bear. The book never explicitly mentions her Blackness, but because it's a picture book and she's the central figure, the children who read it become accustomed to seeing a darker-skinned child as the protagonist.

Next, select books that will introduce complex topics in age-appropriate ways. I'm a big fan of the book *Our Skin: A First Conversation About Race* by Megan Madison, Jessica Ralli, and Isabel Roxas, which teaches about race and racism in a way that's accessible for even the youngest of learners. Finally, books can be a terrific way to help educate your child about different moments in history, often by highlighting lesser-known stories. Mara Rockliff's *Sweet Justice: Georgia Gilmore and the Montgomery Bus Boycott* narrates the story of the Montgomery bus boycott through the lens of a woman who uses her cooking skills to support the movement. And Disney lovers will enjoy Julie Leung's *Paper Son: The Inspiring*

Story of Tyrus Wong, Immigrant and Artist, which chronicles the immigration story of the man who became an illustrator on the film *Bambi.* Books have always been a portal through which we can experience other worlds. Leverage this by selecting stories that illuminate the rich diversity of human experiences and the vast possibilities of what humanity can look like and be.

This framework can also apply to other forms of media. With exposure to diversity as an explicit goal, you may begin guiding your child toward TV shows and movies you might not have previously considered. For example, my toddler, like many, is a huge fan of Ms. Rachel. I was delighted to turn on her program one day and see Jules, a trans, non-binary musician who uses they/them pronouns, as one of the show's rotating guest teachers. Over time, I noticed that Ms. Rachel's videos include a wide range of guests, of all different ethnicities and races. Some engage with their cultural backgrounds—like when Angelo introduces a few Tagalog words—while others simply contribute to the show by virtue of their presence. I was so happy to know that my daughter was getting quality content that *also* sent a powerful message: There are lots of different types of people in the world, and they all have a place here.

Whatever your preferred media is, consider the ways you can use it to foster your child's understanding of diversity and inspire them to celebrate it. The guidance I've provided thus far has focused on preschool-age children because I find that parents are typically less equipped to have those first direct conversations about race with their toddlers. Of course, a child's education about race and racism doesn't end after preschool; on the contrary, parents need to be vigilant—and even relentless—about reinforcing these ideas throughout their kids' formative years. Thankfully, there are myriad organizations dedicated to this work, and the evergreen resources listed at the end of this chapter are designed to support parents in their journey.

INITIATE OPEN AND INTENTIONAL CONVERSATIONS WITH YOUR KIDS ABOUT RACE AND RACISM

We all wish we could show our children a vision of a world in which racial differences are equally valued or celebrated. Yet, the sobering reality is that we do not live in that world. Racism is all around us, and parents who want to raise White children to be more open and accepting of difference will need to proactively engage their children in discussions about *that*, too.

There's no shortage of opportunities to point out racism in the world, but research indicates that White parents are often reluctant to take advantage of them. Indeed, one study found that *63 percent* of White parents refrained from addressing race-related current events (e.g., the murders of Trayvon Martin and Michael Brown, or the Charleston church shooting) with their children between the ages of eight and twelve.[21] The reasons for this reluctance varied. Some parents adopted a laissez-faire attitude—since their *children* didn't raise the subject, the parents chose not to either. Other parents concluded the discussion was unnecessary, without justifying why. But the most frequent explanation parents provided for sidestepping conversations about race-related current events was that it was "too much" for their child to handle "all of the hate in the world."

While these rationales may seem valid at first glance, remember that *it is a uniquely White privilege* to be able to separate discussions about racism from the lived experience of it. Consider four-year-old Evelyn, who returned home from school feeling dejected on the day she didn't receive a stamp. Experiences like this—rejection, exclusion, or devaluation— are all too common for children of color, often prompting a conversation when a concerned parent notices that their child looks sad and asks what's wrong. By contrast, no such conversation would have been initiated in Tanner's house, as Tanner likely went home without giving the interaction a second thought.

Whereas White parents are spared from talking to their twelve-year-olds about racism because "it's too much to handle," twelve-year-olds of color have already had a long introduction to the realities of "all the hate in the world." White parents of White children will never face the unenviable task of consoling the child who comes home heartbroken because of a classmate's or a teacher's comments about their race. They will never have to grapple with the weight of acknowledging their child's experience *as racism,* or with the fear that doing so might shatter their child's sense of safety in the world.

Parents of color routinely navigate this dynamic—overwhelming or not—because they know that their failure to acknowledge racism with their children could prove fatal (as was the case for Tamir Rice, a twelve-year-old Black boy who was murdered by police for playing with a toy gun).[22] Their children's early education necessarily includes conversations about modulating their speech and behavior, distinguishing safe neighborhoods from ones they should avoid, and de-escalating potentially threatening situations. White children may not share these lived experiences, but their ability to detect and combat racial bias requires that they are not shielded from the realities their peers may face.

Children are impressionable, so it's natural for parents to feel uneasy about exposing them to the darkest aspects of humanity. But shielding White children from the realities of race and racism won't spare them from overwhelm, confusion, or pain once they're inevitably forced to confront those harsh realities—and in some cases, it may heighten their distress as they struggle to process difficult truths they were never taught to navigate. When scrolling through social media, your child might happen upon a video of a person of color being beaten by police. They might overhear a cruel racial slur on the playground, or arrive late to an after-school activity because a disruptive social justice protest shut down the street. And they're likely to be utterly shocked and bewildered by what they heard or saw. Having proactive conversations *before* these situations arise can provide your child with a framework to understand these moments, reducing the likelihood that they'll be caught off guard without the tools to critically engage with what they just experienced.

To navigate the delicate balance of informing your children without overwhelming them, find ways to tie the racism they observe or encounter to concepts that are already familiar to them. For example, conversations with toddlers and preschoolers frequently emphasize values such as kindness. With *that* frame, you can describe racism as what happens when some people aren't kind to other people—maybe because they look different or have a different way of speaking. You can then gently remind your child about the ways *they* can practice kindness, like sharing their toys and including everyone during playtime. And you can plant the seeds of allyship by emphasizing that it's *especially* important for your child to be kind when they observe another child who looks lonely and upset.

As your child matures, one way to build on that foundation is to connect the abstract concept of racism to real-world events. For elementary school–age children, when there's a protest happening in your city, you can explain that people are upset because of the unfair treatment a certain group is experiencing. You can remind them that racism is unkind, hurtful, and even cruel, and that people have a right to speak out against it. A conversation at this age will likely be more dynamic than one with a toddler, so don't be afraid to ask your child how *they* feel about what they're seeing and hearing. Answer their questions with honesty—and if they ask a question that you don't know how to answer, make it a joint learning opportunity.

For preteens and teenagers, incorporate a layer of historical context. This can often mean weaving the conversation about racism into what they're already learning. For example, my US history class included lessons about slavery, the Civil War and Reconstruction, and the civil rights movement. Those historical events can readily lend themselves to a conversation about modern policing and the mass incarceration of Black people, the ongoing disenfranchisement of people of color, and present-day racial justice protests. As you ask your child to share what they learned in school that day, link present-day realities to those historical events and lessons. Not only will this give them a richer understanding of what they're learning; it will also help them see that the "past" they're discovering is not so distant after all.

When my niece was in first grade, she came home from school one day incensed by what she had just learned about Thanksgiving. She burst through the door and exclaimed, "Imagine if someone came into our house and told us they decided to live here now and we needed to get out. *That's* what the Pilgrims did to the Native Americans! That's just *wrong!*" Moments like these are opportunities to have frank, productive conversations about how the historical injustices in our nation's past continue to reverberate today.

By tailoring the conversation to your child's age and maturity, you can learn to balance their awareness of racism with their emotional capacity to process it. Make it your goal to provide your White child with adaptive coping mechanisms as they learn more about racism and feel the very real emotions (anxiety, confusion, anger, overwhelm) that accompany their education. Remind them that their actions matter. Invite a conversation about how they can confront and challenge racism and help people from all backgrounds feel safe and welcome. Point out injustices big and small, and ask how they would make changes to promote fairness. This reinforces your child's sense of agency. Teach them that the best way to cope with the disappointment of an unfair world is by taking action to make it better.

DON'T LET (IM)PERFECTION STAND IN YOUR WAY

As I speak with White parents about nurturing egalitarian leanings in their children, I find that they're generally on board with my recommendations about books, media, and even engaging in difficult conversations about racism. Yet there's another obstacle they need support in overcoming: the fear of messing up. This book has largely focused on assisting White adults in identifying bias more effectively, becoming more aware of how racism manifests in the world, the role they may play in maintaining racial hierarchies, and what strategies they can use to combat them. But when I speak with adults who are also parents, I find that this awareness takes an interesting turn: Precisely *because* those adults are aware of how harmful the misguided teachings of their youth were, they are desperate to "get it right" with their children. They know how crucial it is to raise a White child who rejects racial bias—but as a result, they put a lot of pressure on themselves to do it perfectly.

I understand where this pressure comes from. With most things we teach our children—how to tie their shoes, how to do their math homework, how to drive—we want to have mastered the subject before becoming the teacher. But this simply isn't possible when it comes to racism and bias detection—and that's okay. Instead of thinking they can perfect the art of bias detection, our children need to know that the journey is lifelong and ever evolving. When they observe us learning, relearning, and *un*learning over the course of our lives, they develop the patience, perseverance, and curiosity to do the same. Given this, I have one more piece of advice: Do not let the perfect be the enemy of the good.

Emerging evidence suggests that even a clumsy attempt at addressing race with your children is better than nothing. Considering that children pick up on their parents' moods and anxieties, it would be reasonable to presume that if their parents were uncomfortable during a conversation about race, the children would become uncomfortable as well.[23] But one study, in which researchers asked White parents to engage in a guided discussion about racism with their eight-to-twelve-year-old children, revealed that the parents' discomfort (evidenced by how stiff or tense they seemed during the discussion, as well as by biophysical markers like their heart rate) had no bearing at all on their children's attitudes.[24] In the simplest terms, even if the parents were internally panicking during the race-related discussion, their discomfort and anxiety did not undermine their children's learning experience.

The takeaway for White parents here resembles one of my favorite motivational quotes: If you want to do something, *do it*! And if you want to do something that scares you, *do it scared*! Even if you're nervous, anxious, or uncomfortable about talking with your kids about race, *do it anyway*. You may even find that the more you do it, the easier it becomes.

CORRECT YOUR CHILD'S BIASES THROUGH WORDS AND ACTIONS

The tools described here so far are essential for raising children who adopt antibias behaviors as their default—but they alone are not sufficient. There will come a time when parents need to *correct* their children's biases, just as they correct their children's mistakes or undesirable behaviors in so many other arenas of their lives. It can be bewildering to hear our children express biases—especially when those statements or actions deeply contradict our own beliefs—but in those moments, it's useful to remember that children's brains are remarkably malleable. We just need to provide them with new inputs.

At times, we'll have no clue where our children pick up the biases they echo. One day, a passing comment from my niece left my sister and me momentarily speechless. It was the year *The Lego Movie* came out, and my niece offhandedly remarked that she wished she could see the movie but that it was "just for boys." Given that my sister had said nothing of the sort, my niece had clearly internalized a message from *somewhere* (kids at school? Lego ads? another media channel?) that Legos just aren't suitable toys for girls. My sister and I sprang into action: We didn't just *tell* my niece that girls can play with Legos; we *showed* her, too. My sister made sure to take her to *The Lego Movie*, and on my next visit, my niece and I went on a little outing that included getting fresh manicures (our usual ritual) *and* a visit to the Lego store.

Of course, not every biased misstep a child makes has a simple fix—as any parent who's cringed at their child's unfiltered public observations can attest. When your child loudly declares, "That man's skin is really dirty!" about the dark-skinned stranger in front of you in line at the grocery store, staying calm is probably the furthest thing from your mind. (More likely is that you wish the earth would open and swallow you whole to save you from embarrassment.[25]) There are two things happening here, and neither one of them is inherently racist: The child is calling attention to a difference they observe (the darker skin tone), and they are drawing a conclusion based on their own experience (my hands look darker after playing at the park, but they go back to normal once I wash them). You can respect the first part by affirming that the person's skin *is* dark, and you can address the second by clarifying that their skin isn't dirty at all. Some people simply have darker skin, and others have lighter skin. The man in line with you is just one possibility among the endless variations of human appearance. (That said, if the person in question has heard the comment, a quick apology doesn't hurt. Whether or not your child meant any harm by their statement, being called dirty can trigger painful associations for people of color.) Here is a situation in which being proactive in exposing your child to diverse media can help tremendously: A child who has read books and watched TV shows or videos featuring diverse characters, and who has played with dolls or action figures with different skin tones, is less likely to make the "dirty" comment to begin with.

Another important possibility to consider during these corrective moments is a difficult pill to swallow: Sometimes our children's behavior *is* a reflection of our own. Case in point: When my daughter was about a year and a half old, she learned how to say Jackie Sharp, our pet cat's name. We thought it was very cute (it was!). Shortly thereafter, though, we noticed behavior that *wasn't* so cute: She started exclaiming, "*Move,* Jackie!" with a vocal intensity that was surprising for her size and stature. After a few weeks, she began punctuating this stern command with a little (and sometimes not-so-little) swat to move the cat out of her way. My amusement turned to horror as I realized she was clearly mimicking my own behavior. I had often swatted Jackie off of various surfaces while speaking to her in a frustrated tone, and it hadn't taken my toddler long to pick up on this. I realized that if I wanted her behavior to change, I couldn't just correct her—I had to adjust my *own* behavior as well. Immediately, I started showing more affection toward our cat, happily greeting her when she came into the room and pointing out her endearing behaviors to my daughter. When I needed Jackie to move off a surface, I opted for gentler language as I picked her up and placed her on the floor instead of shooing her away like I had in the past. Slowly, my daughter's interactions with Jackie regained their sweet and affectionate tone.

Parents whose children show not-so-flattering racial behaviors need to embrace a similar pattern of introspection. Consider what your child's statements and actions are signaling about the behaviors you've modeled for them, and work to modify *your* behaviors to positively influence *theirs*.

Parents have one of the most difficult jobs in the world, and the reality is that our at-home lessons about equity and inclusion will face considerable competition as our children move out into the world, have their own firsthand experiences, and develop their own attitudes. But that doesn't have to be a bad thing. Throughout this book, I've told stories about children who have positively influenced their *parents'* attitudes—like the children who pointed out their parents' racism after George Floyd's murder, or my own daughter, who showed me that I needed to adjust my own behavior if

I wanted to improve *hers*. Child development experts have long pointed out that while parents shape their children's beliefs and values, children also play a role in shaping their parents' growth.[26] As you engage your child in embracing and celebrating difference, look out for these bidirectional learning opportunities. Like the one-year-old whose unhurried pace can invite even the busiest of adults to *literally* stop and smell the roses, children can encourage the adults in their lives to see the world's racial realities in a different—and better—light.

The best part? This learning reinforces a virtuous cycle: The more you invite your children into conversations about race, the more the conversations about race will happen. The more often you talk about race, the less intimidating the topic will feel. Eventually, you'll be able to have these discussions with greater ease, leading to a more natural give-and-take as you engage your child. Over time, these discussions will become a normal part of your child's reality—and of yours, too.

This process of bidirectional learning and intergenerational dialogue is why I dismiss the ridiculous notion that any single generation will eradicate racism. The children *are* our future, but it would be a mistake to discount the adults who are raising them and modeling for them how to *be* in the world. If *we* commit to creating change—leading with inclusion, embracing acceptance, and being intentional about the messages our children receive—then the future leaders we raise will walk the path we carve for them.

MORE RESOURCES TO SUPPORT YOUR CHILD'S EDUCATION ABOUT RACE AND RACISM

- EmbraceRace has a great guide on where to find diverse children's books: https://www.embracerace.org/resources/where-to-find-diverse-childrens-books
- The Chicago Public Library's Teen Services librarians have curated a list of social justice books for teens: https://chipublib.bibliocommons.com/v2/list/display/200121216/675212937
- We Need Diverse Books is a nonprofit dedicated to exactly what the name says—increasing diverse representation in children's books: https://diversebooks.org/
- PBS Kids for Parents provides articles, videos, and book recommendations geared toward talking about racism with young children (many feature favorite children's characters, like Daniel Tiger and Arthur): https://www.pbs.org/parents/talking-about-racism
- The Center for Racial Justice in Education has a living document of expert interviews, resource lists, and classroom examples to help educators navigate these topics with their students: https://centerracialjustice.org/resources/resources-for-talking-about-race-racism-and-racialized-violence-with-kids/

Conclusion

A CASE FOR OPTIMISM AND
A FINAL CALL TO ACTION

Toward the end of 2021, I was invited to speak on a panel at the Fortune Brainstorm Tech conference.[1] It was my first time attending—let alone speaking at—a conference of this caliber, and I was excited to share my thoughts on how technology could help companies "do well while doing good" to a room full of people who had incredible power to make a difference. Drawing on my professional experience as an executive at a DEI consulting firm, I described the dramatic increase in clients requesting support for their anti-racism efforts that began in the summer of 2020, and I expressed optimism that many of our clients were still committed to that work—even as society's fervor for anti-racist pursuits seemed to be subsiding. I wanted the tech founders and C-suite leaders in our audience to understand that their sustained commitment to this work could meaningfully transform the trajectory of their companies, their employees' lives, their communities, and eventually, the world.

Shortly after the panel, I found myself engaged in a conversation with a journalist who had attended my session.[2] A self-described pessimist, Jonathan was skeptical of the bright picture I painted of the world and wanted to know whether I *really* believed the message of optimism that I shared. He countered my examples of the leaders driving change with his own examples of leaders who were apathetic in the face of inequity, resistant to changing their mindsets, and convinced that their biases were objective, accurate observations—that is to say, not biases at all. He was open to changing his mind and clearly looking to me to help him do so. "Maybe I'm wrong," he said hopefully.

I understood Jonathan's pessimism firsthand—I'd experienced many of the same interactions that led him to question the future of diversity, equity, and inclusion in corporate spaces. However, while Jonathan understood those negative experiences as proof of an unchanging reality, I saw those same apathetic leaders as outliers in a corporate world that was slowly evolving. Instead of dwelling on these negative examples, I was focused on the leaders who were beginning to see that they needed to get off the sidelines, use their voices, and take bold actions to drive change—even in the face of backlash. I had hope for the future because I had seen a spark ignite within so many people, and I had faith that *most* people would nurture that spark into a flame, rather than snuff it out.

In the years since that conversation, I've sometimes struggled to reconcile my more optimistic perspective about the future of racial justice in this country—and in the world in general—with the very troubling realities that we face. As I write this in March 2025, the powers that be (whether that's government leaders, tech bro CEOs, or decision-makers at any level) seem hell-bent on removing essential guardrails that protect marginalized communities from harm, and undermining the very existence of equity-based efforts. Put simply, it's really, really bad—people have already lost jobs, loved ones, and basic human rights—and it's undeniable that there are more dark times ahead. Nevertheless, I still believe that there's a case to be made for optimism.

One of my favorite quotes from Dr. Martin Luther King Jr. comes from a speech he delivered on a few different occasions, perhaps most famously in Washington, DC, on March 31, 1968, just four days before his assassination: "Remaining Awake Through a Great Revolution."[3] Nearly sixty years later, King's message remains strikingly relevant. He spoke of the dangers of isolationism, ongoing racial injustice, and violence and warned his audiences that these struggles would not be resolved anytime soon. And yet, he encouraged his audiences to be *active participants* in the great moments that transform history. He stressed the importance of adopting new mindsets and behaviors to meet the demands of social change. In his closing remarks, he emphasized his own optimism and faith in the future: "We shall overcome," he maintained, "because the arc of the moral universe is long, but it bends toward justice." King didn't believe that things would simply get better with the passage of time; instead, he believed that things would get better because of the tangible actions people would take in the face of injustice.

I'll be the first to admit that racial progress is not linear. But as I reflect upon the current state of affairs, I'm reminded of example after example of people who are not shirking the responsibility of fighting injustice; instead, they're taking concrete steps to steer the arc of the moral universe toward justice. In response to the revocation of basic human rights like the right to bodily autonomy, company leaders are updating their healthcare offerings and travel policies and halting plans for expansion into cities and states that do not align with their inclusive values. In response to large-scale attacks on diversity, equity, and inclusion initiatives, organizations are strengthening their commitment to DEI work and inclusive hiring. Meanwhile, people are coming together to create coalitions built on the intersections of marginalized identities, channel resources to the communities that need them most, and drive change at every level. Librarians are resisting censorship by keeping banned books on their shelves. Millions are donating to legal aid funds to support protesters fighting injustice. Others are toppling statues and removing symbols that glorify the Confederacy. These are not perfect solutions to the systemic inequity running rampant in our country, but it *is* heartening to see people from all races and identities—and especially those from more privileged backgrounds—working within their spheres of influence toward a common goal.

Each of us has a role to play in shaping the just moral universe we envision, and research shows that meaningful action has driven some of the most significant shifts in attitudes toward marginalized groups.[4] When people adopt new mindsets and behaviors to meet the demands of social change—just as King called for—beliefs change, laws are rewritten, and our world becomes a better place.

It's up to you to choose your level of investment in this process. In the year or two following George Floyd's murder, I had many a conversation with White people who moaned that the pursuit of inclusion and anti-racism was "tiring" and "not fun anymore." They complained that there hadn't been more progress over the past two years and wondered how much more they would have to endure before being able to move on to something else. Despite my reminders that people of color do *not* have the privilege of taking a break from eradicating racism—our survival depends on it—some of the White people I spoke with ultimately retreated from their anti-racism efforts and disengaged from conversations about race. But I also spoke with *so many more* White people who made a different choice. These people doubled down on their commitment to being active participants in combating racial bias. They recognized that undoing centuries of bias requires persistence and commitment. They understood the power of their role—whether it was calling out a friend's biased remark or sharing a thought-provoking book with a skeptical coworker. They acknowledged their White privilege and opted to "share their candy" by turning down an opportunity, suggesting a person of color who'd be a great fit (but may not have come to mind as quickly) for the job instead.

I don't think it's possible to do this work—the work of dismantling racism—without the belief that things can get better. Thankfully, those transformative experiences I've witnessed fuel my optimism and are what inspired me to write this book, to help educate more people and provide concrete strategies for detecting and combating bias at scale. If we collectively take responsibility for calling out bias—questioning how our families, workplaces, and communities can improve, and actively working toward that vision—change will follow. I recognize that there will be setbacks, and that not everyone will get on board. But many more *will*, and together, we are shaping the consciousness of all those around us.

Most importantly, I know that *you*—now at the end of this book—are yet another person who will be equipped to join the fight and help ensure that the arc of the moral universe bends toward justice. To me, that is something to be optimistic about.

Acknowledgments

An Instagram post changed my life. In April 2023, I was doing my usual scrolling, and I came across a post from Little, Brown Spark announcing a call for book submissions. The New Voices Award was a partnership between Little, Brown Spark and Psychotherapy Networker, inviting psychologists from underrepresented backgrounds to submit a nonfiction book proposal. As I read the details, I did a double take. I was a *perfect fit*, so much so that I thought I was dreaming, or on the receiving end of some very elaborate prank. I still cannot believe all the things that have happened in the two-plus years since that day. It feels downright magical to have my first book (yay!) published and out in the world. So my first acknowledgment goes to Little, Brown Spark, Psychotherapy Networker, and the brains behind the New Voices Award. Thank you for recognizing that we need more authors from underrepresented backgrounds, thank you for recognizing the barriers to that more diverse reality, and thank you for creating a viable pathway for authors like me.

Acknowledgments

My husband, champion, and first reader—James, thank you for your constant encouragement, your helpful feedback, and your willingness to drop everything to read edit upon edit of each chapter *right now*. Your voice drowns out the doubts in my head, and you hold me up even in the face of my most self-sabotaging tendencies. Thank you for making sure I hit submit on that call for proposals and for carrying the weight of our growing family as I wrote this book.

My village—To my parents, thank you for instilling the values that set me on my research, and now writing, journey. You both believed I had ideas worth sharing with the world long before this book came to fruition. I hope the stories from my childhood and adulthood woven throughout this text honor all you've poured into me. To my friends Evan and Christina, you both said yes to helping me with childcare on such short notice, without which I would not have finished the book proposal. Thank you for letting me lean on you (and thank you to Luca for his patience during Georgia's play-date!). Ms. Dobson, Glenn, and Grace, thank you each for your thoughtful close reads of the first full draft of this book. Your feedback and excitement helped me feel more confident and excited about what I had created.

To my research collaborators—It has been thrilling to translate the research we have conducted into this book. I am so proud of the work we have done together, and I hope its inclusion here leads more people to seek out, and to value, basic and applied research. A special note of gratitude to Sam Sommers and Mike Norton: Your 2006 lay theories paper ignited my passion for using research to answer big questions about racism. While I have not published with either of you, I have still felt, and benefited from, the impact of your ideas in our field. Sam, you are deeply missed. Finally, thank you to the named and unnamed people whose stories are included in this book. We are all always learning and growing, and you clearly had a profound impact on me. I hope that my retelling of our conversations will prove insightful for my readers as well.

My editing and agent team—Talia, from our very first conversation I knew I would be able to trust you to help bring this book to life. Your open communication, your honesty—whether for praise or critique—and your accessibility are just a few of the traits that make you an exceptional editor. Thank you for championing this book and for shepherding me through my first publishing process. Lauren, in chapter 5 I write about the powerful role of a birth doula; here is where I acknowledge the powerful role of the *book* doula as well. You polished my prose and made the words sing on the page, all while protecting my voice and style. I still marvel that our professional relationship years ago turned into this wonderful partnership. Lynn, you understood early on what made my book unique, even when other agents saw "another DEI book." Thank you for your expert guidance and advocacy. I am thrilled to have found you.

The publishing powerhouse that is Little, Brown Spark— I have long been a fan of yours. The titles published under this imprint do, indeed, "spark an idea, a feeling, a change," and I

Acknowledgments

am glad my book has found a home under this banner. I am filled with immense gratitude for the entire team responsible for making the books at this imprint happen, including those I have interacted with directly and indirectly. A special note of thanks to the cover artist, who nailed it on the first try. We need books that make people uncomfortable. We need books that challenge people to change their mindsets and to become better humans. And we need publishers willing to publish those books even, and especially, when some deem the ideas within them unpopular. Thank you for your unwavering commitment to that goal.

Notes

Chapter 1: Growth Mindset and the Practice of Detecting Racial Bias

1. Ericsson, K. A., Krampe, R. T., & Tesch-Römer, C. (1993). The role of deliberate practice in the acquisition of expert performance. *Psychological Review, 100*(3), 363–406. https://doi.org/10.1037/0033-295X.100.3.363

2. Dweck, C. S. (2006). *Mindset: The new psychology of success.* Random House, p. 12.

3. Dweck, 2006, p. 11.

4. Dweck, C. S., & Leggett, E. L. (1988). A social-cognitive approach to motivation and personality. *Psychological Review, 95*(2), 256–273. https://doi.org/10.1037/0033-295X.95.2.256

5. The verses of the song "Growth Mindset" by Numberock include catchy rhymes like "You won't quit or give up, even when it gets rough, because your mind can take on tasks that seem tough!" and "It's OK to mess up a little, here or there; it's learning from mistakes that takes you anywhere." The chorus drives this point home with its thematic refrain: "Instead of saying 'I can't' say 'I can't yet.' All it takes to make it is a growth mindset!" Math Songs by Numberock. (2018, August 7). "Growth Mindset Songs for Kids" [Video]. YouTube. https://www.youtube.com/watch?v=0roRXBlEuRs

6. Festinger, L. (1957). *A theory of cognitive dissonance.* Stanford University Press.

7. Goldstein, D. (2020, January 12). Two states. Eight textbooks. Two American stories. *New York Times.* https://www.nytimes.com/interactive/2020/01/12/us/texas-vs-california-history-textbooks.html

8. Carr, P. B., Dweck, C. S., & Pauker, K. (2012). Beliefs about the malleability of prejudice: Implications for intergroup conflict. *Journal of Personality and Social Psychology, 104*(6), 1029–1049. https://doi.org/10.1037/a0029743

9. Bergsieker, H. B., Shelton, J. N., & Richeson, J. A. (2010). To be liked versus respected: Divergent goals in interracial interactions. *Journal of Personality and Social Psychology, 99*(2), 248–264. https://doi.org/10.1037/a0018474

10. Researchers have actually quantified the extent to which this is true. In one study assessing attitudes toward different groups, the only groups more hated than "racists" were terrorists, wife beaters, child molesters, child abusers, and rapists. Crandall, C. S., Eshleman, A., & O'Brien, L. (2002). Social norms and the expression and suppression of prejudice: The struggle for internalization. *Journal of Personality and Social Psychology, 82*(3), 359–378. https://doi.org/10.1037/0022-3514.82.3.359

11. Using fake articles to nudge participants' beliefs in one direction or another is a common researcher practice, in part because people are generally quite willing to consider new information, especially when it comes from a source they deem reputable. This susceptibility to suggestion is why researchers must go through a rigorous ethical review process before beginning any study. Moreover, any study that involves deception, as this one did, requires a full debriefing at the end. That is, the research team must explain to the participants all manner of deception used, as well as the hypotheses of the study, and give them a chance to ask questions; debriefing serves as a "reset to factory settings" conversation of sorts.

12. Bergelson, I., Tracy, C., & Takacs, E. (2022). Best practices for reducing bias in the interview process. *Current Urology Reports, 23*(11), 319–325; Bohnet, I. (2016, April 18). How to take the bias out of job interviews. *Harvard Business Review.* https://hbr.org/2016/04/how-to-take-the-bias-out-of-job-interviews; Dipboye, R. L. (1994). Structured and unstructured selection interviews: Beyond the job-fit model. *Research in Personnel and Human Resources Management, 12,* 79–123.

13. Both names have been changed.

Notes

Chapter 2: The Gift of Fear

1. Eysenck, M. W., Derakshan, N., Santos, R., & Calvo, M. G. (2007). Anxiety and cognitive performance: Attentional control theory. *Emotion, 7*(2), 336–353. https://doi.org/10.1037/1528-3542.7.2.336

2. Richeson, J. A., Trawalter, S., & Shelton, J. N. (2005). African Americans' implicit racial attitudes and the depletion of executive function. *Personality and Social Psychology Bulletin, 31*(9), 1044–1056. https://doi.org/10.1177/0146167205274855; Murphy, M. C., Richeson, J. A., Shelton, J. N., Rheinschmidt, M. L., & Bergsieker, H. B. (2013). Cognitive costs of contemporary prejudice. *Group Processes & Intergroup Relations, 16*(5), 560–571. https://doi.org/10.1177/1368430212468170

3. Richeson, J. A., & Shelton, J. N. (2003). When prejudice does not pay: Effects of interracial contact on executive function. *Psychological Science, 14*(3), 287–290.

4. DiAngelo, R. (2018). *White fragility: Why it's so hard for White people to talk about racism.* Beacon Press; Ford, B. Q., Green, D. J., & Gross, J. J. (2022). White fragility: An emotion regulation perspective. *American Psychologist, 77*(4), 510.

5. DiAngelo, R., & Sensoy, Ö. (2014). Getting slammed: White depictions of race discussions as arenas of violence. *Race Ethnicity and Education, 17*(1), 103–128. https://doi.org/10.1080/13613324.2013.832919

6. Jackson, R., & Rao, S. (2022). *White women: Everything you already know about your own racism and how to do better.* Penguin Books.

7. Anderson, C. (2016). *White rage: The unspoken truth of our racial divide.* Bloomsbury Publishing.

8. Deci, E. L., & Ryan, R. M. (2013). Self-determination theory. In E. Kessler (Ed.), *Encyclopedia of management theory* (pp. 686–690). Sage Publications; Teixeira, P. J., Carraça, E. V., Markland, D., Silva, M. N., & Ryan, R. M. (2012). Exercise, physical activity, and self-determination theory: A systematic review. *International Journal of Behavioral Nutrition and Physical Activity, 9*, 78. https://doi.org/10.1186/1479-5868-9-78

9. Legault, L., Gutsell, J. N., & Inzlicht, M. (2011). Ironic effects of anti-prejudice messages: How motivational interventions can reduce (but also increase) prejudice. *Psychological Science, 22*(12), 1472–1477. https://doi.org/10.1177/0956797611416255

Notes

10. Monteith, M. J., Parker, L. R., & Burns, M. D. (2016). The self-regulation of prejudice. In T. D. Nelson (Ed.), *Handbook of stereotyping, prejudice, and discrimination* (pp. 409–432). Psychology Press.

Chapter 3: Racial Bias Can Be Subtle

1. At the time, the National Museum of African American History and Culture was still just a dream that advocates were working to make a reality. I didn't get to visit for the first time until years later as an adult; however, I experienced a thrilling full-circle moment when my "bonus daughter" (the phrase we use instead of "stepdaughter") visited the museum on *her* eighth-grade DC trip.

2. Sommers, S. R., & Norton, M. I. (2006). Lay theories about White racists: What constitutes racism (and what doesn't)? *Group Processes & Intergroup Relations, 9*(1), 117–138. https://doi.org/10.1177/1368430206059881

3. It's worth noting that, while things have certainly improved, norms are fragile and susceptible to change—especially in the form of backsliding. A 2018 study found that President Trump's bigoted rhetoric during the 2016 US presidential election ushered in such a lapse. Specifically, participants thought it was more acceptable to express bias against groups targeted by Trump rhetoric (e.g., Asian Americans, disabled people, and immigrants) *after* the election than they did *before*. We cannot assume an arc of ongoing progress—that biased attitudes necessarily disappear with time. We must actively, and continuously, work to identify and root out bias if we want to see *sustained* change. Crandall, C. S., Miller, J. M., & White, M. H. (2018). Changing norms following the 2016 US presidential election: The Trump effect on prejudice. *Social Psychological and Personality Science, 9*(2), 186–192.

4. Roberts, S. O., & Rizzo, M. T. (2021). The psychology of American racism. *American Psychologist, 76*(3), 475.

5. The idea that having a more diverse pool of candidates necessarily means that one must have lower standards for whom should be hired (i.e., "lower the bar") is one of the most oft-repeated phrases within corporate spaces. Framing a racist belief that people of color are inherently less qualified than White people as a pursuit of "the best" is offensive and inaccurate. Compared to White people, people of color are typically scrutinized

Notes

more and *held* to higher standards. If anything, the all-White talent pools are a hindrance to truly finding the best talent.

6. Clark, R., Anderson, N. B., Clark, V. R., & Williams, D. R. (1999). Racism as a stressor for African Americans: A biopsychosocial model. *American Psychologist, 54*(10), 805.

7. This definition is an amalgamation of definitions used by scholars like Derald Wing Sue, who first introduced the term *microaggressions,* and other scholars who have adapted and refined the definition in an attempt to most comprehensively describe these fleeting, yet quite harmful, experiences. Lewis, J. A., & Neville, H. A. (2015). Construction and initial validation of the Gendered Racial Microaggressions Scale for Black women. *Journal of Counseling Psychology, 62*(2), 289; O'Keefe, V. M., Wingate, L. R., Cole, A. B., Hollingsworth, D. W., & Tucker, R. P. (2015). Seemingly harmless racial communications are not so harmless: Racial microaggressions lead to suicidal ideation by way of depression symptoms. *Suicide and Life-Threatening Behavior, 45*(5), 567–576; Pearson, A. R., Dovidio, J. F., & Gaertner, S. L. (2009). The nature of contemporary prejudice: Insights from aversive racism. *Social and Personality Psychology Compass, 3*(3), 314–338; Sue, D. W., Capodilupo, C. M., Torino, G. C., Bucceri, J. M., Holder, A., Nadal, K. L., & Esquilin, M. (2007). Racial microaggressions in everyday life: Implications for clinical practice. *American Psychologist, 62*(4), 271; Wong, G., Derthick, A. O., David, E. J. R., Saw, A., & Okazaki, S. (2014). The what, the why, and the how: A review of racial microaggressions research in psychology. *Race and Social Problems, 6*, 181–200.

8. Castilla, E. J., & Benard, S. (2010). The paradox of meritocracy in organizations. *Administrative Science Quarterly, 55*(4), 543–676.

9. This is a universal phenomenon. Résumé audit studies from around the world show how consistently societal biases show up in the hiring process. A few examples: In the United States, the exact same résumé gets 50 percent more callbacks for an interview if the name at the top is Emily or Greg (suggesting that the candidate is White) than if the name is Lakisha or Jamal (suggesting that the candidate is Black). In China, having a Han name provides a considerable advantage compared to having a Mongolian, Uighur, or Tibetan name. In Canada, applicants

with English-sounding names fare better than those with Chinese, Indian, or Pakistani names. Finally, a 2024 analysis in the *New York Times* highlighted the persistence of this phenomenon. Bertrand, M., & Mullainathan, S. (2004). Are Emily and Greg more employable than Lakisha and Jamal? A field experiment on labor market discrimination. *American Economic Review, 94*(4), 991–1013; Maurer-Fazio, M. (2012). Ethnic discrimination in China's internet job board labor market. *IZA Journal of Migration, 1,* 1–24; Oreopoulos, P. (2011). Why do skilled immigrants struggle in the labor market? A field experiment with thirteen thousand résumés. *American Economic Journal: Economic Policy, 3*(4), 148–171; Miller, C. C., & Katz, J. (2024, April 8). What researchers discovered when they sent 80,000 fake résumés to US jobs. *New York Times.* https://www.nytimes.com/2024/04/08/upshot /employment-discrimination-fake-resumes.html

10. Kang, S. K., DeCelles, K. A., Tilcsik, A., & Jun, S. (2016). Whitened résumés: Race and self-presentation in the labor market. *Administrative Science Quarterly, 61*(3), 469–502. https://doi.org/10.1177 /0001839216639577

11. Hodson, G., Dovidio, J. F., & Gaertner, S. L. (2002). Processes in racial discrimination: Differential weighting of conflicting information. *Personality and Social Psychology Bulletin, 28*(4), 460–471. https://doi .org/10.1177/0146167202287004

12. Feagin, J. R., & Sikes, M. P. (1994). *Living with racism: The Black middle-class experience.* Beacon Press, p. 282.

13. Ninety-five percent of the participants in this study were White. Kaiser, C. R., & Miller, C. T. (2001). Stop complaining! The social costs of making attributions to discrimination. *Personality and Social Psychology Bulletin, 27*(2), 254–263.

14. You may be thinking that there are any number of alternative explanations for these results. For example, maybe the person was more endearing when he took responsibility for his low score compared to when he blamed it on external factors, thus the "complainer" label was not about a discrimination attribution, per se, but about a dislike for eschewing personal responsibility. To that end, in a subsequent study by the same authors, the researchers compared judgments about a Black person who blamed his low grade on answer quality, discrimination, and

test difficulty. Although the latter two attributions were both external, only the person who attributed his low score to discrimination was judged to be a complainer. Kaiser, C. R., Dyrenforth, P. S., & Hagiwara, N. (2006). Why are attributions to discrimination interpersonally costly? A test of system- and group-justifying motivations. *Personality and Social Psychology Bulletin, 32*(11), 1423–1536.

15. Kaiser, C. R., & Miller, C. T. (2003). Derogating the victim: The interpersonal consequences of blaming events on discrimination. *Group Processes & Intergroup Relations, 6*(3), 227–237.

16. Diebels, K. J., & Czopp, A. M. (2011). Complaining about a compliment: Evaluating attributions of positive outcomes to discrimination. *Asian Journal of Social Psychology, 14*(3), 217–223.

17. Howard, S., Kennedy, K., & Tejeda, F. (2020). Social media posts about racism leads to evaluative backlash for Black job applicants. *Social Media+ Society, 6*(4), 2056305120978369.

18. Chappelle, D., Rock, C., Brennan, N., Jost, C., & Tucker, B. (Writers). (2016, November 12). "Election Night" [Video]. *Saturday Night Live*. NBC.

19. Tumblr. (2014). "I, Too, Am Harvard." https://itooamharvard.tumblr.com /archive

20. Carter, E. R. (2015). Strength in numbers?: Effects of exposure to multiple claims of discrimination [Doctoral dissertation, Indiana University]. ProQuest; Carter, E. R., & Murphy, M. C. (2017). Consensus and consistency: Exposure to multiple discrimination claims shapes Whites' intergroup attitudes. *Journal of Experimental Social Psychology, 73*, 24–33.

21. Kaiser, C. R., Drury, B. J., Spalding, K. E., Cheryan, S., & O'Brien, L. T. (2009). The ironic consequences of Obama's election: Decreased support for social justice. *Journal of Experimental Social Psychology, 45*(3), 556–559; Norton, M. I., & Sommers, S. R. (2011). Whites see racism as a zero-sum game that they are now losing. *Perspectives on Psychological Science, 6*(3), 215–218.

22. In 2015, a demographic survey conducted by the international professional organization Society for Personality and Social Psychology (SPSP) showed that just 3 percent of all social and personality psychologists were Black.

23. A considerable amount of care went into making sure the two research assistants would do this well. First I provided them with definitions of subtle and blatant bias, and some examples of each. Then they spent

some time practicing categorizing the essays, both to understand the task and to align with one another. After they reached an acceptable rate of agreement, they moved on to categorizing actual essays from the study participants. In the rare cases where there was a disagreement between the two, a third person came in as a tiebreaker.

24. West, K. (2019). Testing hypersensitive responses: Ethnic minorities are not more sensitive to microaggressions, they just experience them more frequently. *Personality and Social Psychology Bulletin, 45*(11), 1659–1673. https://doi.org/10.1177/0146167219838790

25. See, e.g., Inbar, Y., & Lammers, J. (2012). Political diversity in social and personality psychology. *Perspectives on Psychological Science, 7*(5), 496–503. https://doi.org/10.1177/1745691612448792

Chapter 4: "White" *Is* a Racial Identity

1. Name has been changed.

2. In the process of writing this chapter, I went back to the list to review the methodology. To a certain extent, the judges *did* consider the racial makeup of each town, although the threshold was quite generous: Only cities that were more than 95 percent White were excluded from consideration. Jennifer's hometown passed this bar, though its racial demographics still don't scream "racially diverse" as far as I'm concerned. As of the 2000 US census, 90.7 percent of city residents were White; in the 2010 US census, 81.7 percent of city residents were White.

3. I still haven't forgiven the city of Dedham, Massachusetts, for making me miss the 2008 BET Awards for this very reason.

4. One time, when I lived in Indiana, I was desperately craving Thai, and I went to the *one* Thai restaurant in town. I ordered a noodle dish with a spice level at the midpoint of the restaurant's scale, expecting to have a dish with the subtle heat that I was accustomed to. But when my food arrived, I was so disappointed—it barely had any kick at all, and it was practically sweet. I learned that the restaurant regularly received complaints from White patrons about the food being "too spicy," so the dishes were adjusted to be more pleasing to their palate. From that point on, I learned to order a couple of levels higher on any restaurant's spice scale just to make sure I got the heat level I wanted (though this was a habit I *quickly* reversed when I moved to Los Angeles and had my first encounter with "Thai spicy"!).

Notes

5. Northwestern is, and always has been, a predominantly White institution. During the year Jennifer and I had this conversation, the undergraduate student population was 6.5 percent Black, 7.8 percent Hispanic, 0.2 percent American Indian, and 21.6 percent Asian American. The following year, a report on the state of diversity at the school compared these data to the US demographics and concluded, "It is immediately apparent that NU enrollments are seriously lagging behind the US population for African American and Latino/a young adults." Northwestern University. (2014). *University diversity and inclusion report 2013–14*. Northwestern University. https://www.northwestern.edu/diversity/docs/university-diversity-and-inclusion-report-2013-14.pdf

6. As of the 2000 and 2010 US censuses, the Black population in each city was as follows: Atlanta (61 percent, 53 percent), Washington, DC (59 percent, 50 percent), and Houston (25.3 percent, 24.7 percent).

7. Greenwald, A. G., & Pettigrew, T. F. (2014). With malice toward none and charity for some: Ingroup favoritism enables discrimination. *American Psychologist, 69*(7), 669–684. https://doi.org/10.1037/a0036056

8. One study found that White participants were more likely to associate White Americans (compared to Black or Asian Americans) with the concept of American. Interestingly, while Asian American participants also showed this "American = White" effect, Black American participants did not. There are many possible reasons for this; perhaps Black Americans were making a *relative* comparison of "Americanness" between their racial group and others that are not indigenous to the United States. Furthermore, in their studies, the researchers characterized "Americanness" as a combination of three traits: patriotism, egalitarianism, and nativeness. Black American participants were more likely to rate their group as higher on the latter two dimensions than White or Asian Americans. Both possibilities would explain why Black American participants were less likely to demonstrate the "American = White" effect than the other participants. Devos, T., & Banaji, M. R. (2005). American = White? *Journal of Personality and Social Psychology, 88*(3), 447–466. https://doi.org/10.1037/0022-3514.88.3.447

9. Fans of the movie *The Best Man Holiday* may remember a *USA Today* story that described the Christmas movie, which features an all-Black cast, with exactly this "race-themed" label.

245

Notes

10. Apfelbaum, E. P., Norton, M. I., & Sommers, S. R. (2012). Racial color blindness: Emergence, practice, and implications. *Current Directions in Psychological Science, 21*(3), 205–209.

11. Even the "melting pot" moniker pointed to a color-blind ideology, suggesting that as people from different cultures and experiences came to the United States, they would blend in.

12. At the time, the Seattle School District was using a racial tiebreaker to ensure the demographics of each school reflected the demographics of the district, which was 41 percent White and 59 percent non-White. For schools where the enrollment deviated too far from the district's demographic, students whose race (either White or non-White) would help bring the racial balance closer to the goal were favored for admission. Ultimately, the US Supreme Court ruled that this practice was unconstitutional. *Parents Involved in Community Schools v. Seattle School District No. 1*, 551 U.S. 701 (2007).

13. The law school curriculum is rife with land mines for students from a variety of backgrounds. In just the first year, students cover how predatory contracts were permitted (contract law), discuss adverse possession, which conveniently justified dispossession of land from Native Americans (property law), and debate the merits of the three-fifths rule for slaves (constitutional law).

14. To say we make a guess is not always to say that we are right. Ultimately, our initial judgments (and actions based on those judgments) of people are based on stereotypes. The nuance of any conversation about identity is that, as we become more comfortable talking about and acknowledging identity, we also need to become more comfortable with challenging our assumptions of how any particular identity is "supposed" to look. Stangor, C., Lynch, L., Duan, C., & Glas, B. (1992). Categorization of individuals on the basis of multiple social features. *Journal of Personality and Social Psychology, 62*(2), 207; Xie, S. Y., Flake, J. K., Stolier, R. M., Freeman, J. B., & Hehman, E. (2021). Facial impressions are predicted by the structure of group stereotypes. *Psychological Science, 32*(12), 1979–1993.

15. In the process of writing this chapter, I unsuccessfully tried to find that transformative article. Although that particular story is lost somewhere on the internet, there are plenty of other accounts of this experience,

including Stacy Bias's *Flying While Fat* animated documentary film. (You can watch it at https://flyingwhilefat.com.)

16. Florida's 2022 Stop WOKE Act is one example of this. It bans workplace training and school instruction that suggest individuals are "inherently racist, sexist, or oppressive, whether consciously or unconsciously." It also prohibits teaching that people are privileged or disadvantaged based on race, gender, or national origin, or that a person "bears personal responsibility for and must feel guilt, anguish, or other forms of psychological distress" over actions committed in the past by members of the same race, gender, or national origin. Since the introduction of this act, similar efforts have proliferated across the country, ranging from K–12 domains to higher education to private workplaces.

17. Brannon, T. N., Carter, E. R., Murdock-Perriera, L. A., & Higginbotham, G. D. (2018). From backlash to inclusion for all: Instituting diversity efforts to maximize benefits across group lines. *Social Issues and Policy Review, 12*(1), 57–90.

18. Eibach, R. P., & Ehrlinger, J. (2006). "Keep your eyes on the prize": Reference points and racial differences in assessing progress toward equality. *Personality and Social Psychology Bulletin, 32*(1), 66–77; see also Kraus, M. W., Onyeador, I. N., Daumeyer, N. M., Rucker, J. M., & Richeson, J. A. (2019). The misperception of racial economic inequality. *Perspectives on Psychological Science, 14*(6), 899–921; Onyeador, I. N., Daumeyer, N. M., Rucker, J. M., Duker, A., Kraus, M. W., & Richeson, J. A. (2021). Disrupting beliefs in racial progress: Reminders of persistent racism alter perceptions of past, but not current, racial economic equality. *Personality and Social Psychology Bulletin, 47*(5), 753–765.

19. Norton, M. I., & Sommers, S. R. (2011). Whites see racism as a zero-sum game that they are now losing. *Perspectives on Psychological Science, 6*(3), 215–218.

20. Hans Christian Andersen was a White Danish author, so it makes sense that his reference for Ariel would be a White woman. Conversely, *Once on This Island* is a musical adaptation of the same story, but because the tale is set in the Caribbean, Ti Moune (the Ariel analog) is a Black woman.

21. Planas, A. (2023, July 20). New Florida standards teach Black people benefited from slavery, taught useful skills. NBC News. https://www

.nbcnews.com/news/us-news/new-florida-standards-teach-black-people
-benefited-slavery-taught-usef-rcna95418

22. Craig, M. A., Rucker, J. M., & Richeson, J. A. (2018). The pitfalls and promise of increasing racial diversity: Threat, contact, and race relations in the 21st century. *Current Directions in Psychological Science, 27*(3), 188–193.

23. Mutz, D. C. (2018). Status threat, not economic hardship, explains the 2016 presidential vote. *Proceedings of the National Academy of Sciences of the United States of America, 115*(19), E4330–E4339.

24. The core focus of the analysis was how the racial makeup of friend groups related to respondents' religious attitudes, but the revelation of the homogeneity of White people's friendship networks was understandably a major takeaway. Cox, D., Navarro-Rivera, J., & Jones, R. P. (2016, August 3). Race, religion, and political affiliation of Americans' core social networks. Public Religion Research Institute. https://www.prri.org /research/poll-race-religion-politics-americans-social-networks/

25. Public Religion Research Institute. (2022, May 24). American bubbles: Politics, race, and religion in Americans' core friendship networks. Public Religion Research Institute. https://www.prri.org/research /american-bubbles-politics-race-and-religion-in-americans-core -friendship-networks/

26. Take note that I, a Black woman, can still fall prey to the White default. Because it is the dominant ideology of our society, *any* person of *any* race can, at times, uphold this standard.

27. Neel, R., & Shapiro, J. R. (2012). Is racial bias malleable? Whites' lay theories of racial bias predict divergent strategies for interracial interactions. *Journal of Personality and Social Psychology, 103*(1), 101.

28. I don't provide specific recommendations for social media accounts to follow because the landscape changes so quickly that such a list would fast become outdated. Instead, I recommend using the practices described in this section to find the accounts that work for you, and to review every so often whether you still find the information shared there to be valuable.

29. Thanks to my mother, Anne Carter, for imparting the definition of diversity as "the differences that make us unique" to me during my formative years.

Notes

Chapter 5: The Magnitude of White Privilege

1. Centers for Disease Control and Prevention. (2024, April 8). *Working together to reduce Black maternal mortality.* US Department of Health & Human Services.

2. Associated Press. (2022, May 9). Family of Black woman who died after "sloppy" C-section sues hospital for racism. *Today.* https://www.today.com/parents/parents/black-woman-died-c-section-racism-lawsuit-cedars-sinai-rcna28029

3. A 2023 review of the available research on the impact of doulas found a whole host of benefits, including positive delivery outcomes (a reduction in C-sections, premature deliveries, and length of labor) and overall reduced anxiety and stress for the birthing parent. Furthermore, studies have found that doulas are especially impactful in mitigating the negative outcomes that contribute to maternal health disparities between White women and women of color. During pregnancy, birth, and the postpartum period, doulas provide a highly involved and customized level of care that is unmatched by the traditional medical system. For example, my doula came to my house each month to lead one-on-one hour-long prenatal dance classes, connected me with a lactation consultant to support my breastfeeding goals, and memorized my birth plan. By contrast, my medical appointments with my OB consisted of a ten-minute in-room visit, and despite all the effort I put into picking her, the person who ended up delivering my daughter was someone I had never met. By providing continuous, one-on-one support throughout and beyond pregnancy, doulas can help advocate for women of color in a system that is designed to ignore us. Sobczak, A., Taylor, L., Solomon, S., Ho, J., Phillips, B., Jacobson, K., ... & Kemper, S. R. (2023). The effect of doulas on maternal and birth outcomes: A scoping review. *Cureus, 15*(5); Stryker, D. (2023, May 10). The role of doulas in addressing Black women's maternal mortality. *Women's Health Education Program Blog, Drexel University College of Medicine.* https://drexel.edu/medicine/academics/womens-health-and-leadership/womens-health-education-program/whep-blog/role-of-doulas-in-addressing-black-womens-maternal-mortality/

Notes

4. Williams, S. (2022, April 5). How Serena Williams saved her own life. *Elle.* https://www.elle.com/life-love/a39586444/how-serena-williams -saved-her-own-life/

5. Aggarwal, P., Brandon, A., Goldszmidt, A., Holz, J., List, J. A., Muir, I.,...& Yu, T. (2022). High-frequency location data shows that race affects the likelihood of being stopped and fined for speeding. University of Chicago, Becker Friedman Institute for Economics Working Paper (2022-160); Wylie, J., Milless, K. L., Sciarappo, J., & Gantman, A. (2024). The biased enforcement of rarely followed rules. *Personality and Social Psychology Bulletin,* 01461672241252853.

6. Reeves, A. N. (2014, April 1). *Written in Black & White: Exploring confirmation bias in racialized perceptions of writing skills.* Nextions. https: //nextions.com/insights/perspectives/written-in-black-white-exploring -confirmation-bias-in-racialized-perceptions-of-writing-skills/

7. Hodson, G., Dovidio, J. F., & Gaertner, S. L. (2002). Processes in racial discrimination: Differential weighting of conflicting information. *Personality and Social Psychology Bulletin, 28*(4), 460–471; Player, A., Randsley de Moura, G., Leite, A. C., Abrams, D., & Tresh, F. (2019). Overlooked leadership potential: The preference for leadership potential in job candidates who are men vs. women. *Frontiers in Psychology, 10,* 391596.

8. Banaji, M. R., Fiske, S. T., & Massey, D. S. (2021). Systemic racism: Individuals and interactions, institutions and society. *Cognitive Research: Principles and Implications, 6*(1), 82.

9. Yearby, R. (2020). Structural racism and health disparities: Re-configuring the social determinants of health framework to include the root cause. *Journal of Law, Medicine & Ethics, 48*(3), 518–526. https: //doi.org/10.1177/1073110520958876

10. Jackson, G. (2019, November 13). The female problem: How male bias in medical trials ruined women's health. *The Guardian.* https://www .theguardian.com/lifeandstyle/2019/nov/13/the-female-problem -male-bias-in-medical-trials

11. Gilmer, G., Hettinger, Z. R., Tuakli-Wosornu, Y., Skidmore, E., Silver, J. K., Thurston, R. C., Lowe, D. A., Ambrosio, F., & Kautz, D. (2023). Female aging: When translational models don't translate. *Nature Aging, 3*(12), 1500–1508. https://doi.org/10.1038/s43587-023-00509-8

Notes

12. Alegria, M., Sud, S., Steinberg, B. E., Gai, N., & Siddiqui, A. (2021). Reporting of participant race, sex, and socioeconomic status in randomized clinical trials in general medical journals, 2015 vs 2019. *JAMA Network Open, 4*(5), e2111516. https://doi.org/10.1001/jamanetworkopen.2021.11516

13. One study found that diseases that primarily affect men were more likely to get research funding from the US National Institutes of Health compared to diseases that primarily affect women. Mirin, A. A. (2021). Gender disparity in the funding of diseases by the US National Institutes of Health. *Journal of Women's Health, 30*(7), 956–963. https://doi.org/10.1089/jwh.2020.8682)

14. Association of American Medical Colleges. (2019). *Diversity in medicine: Facts and figures 2019.* https://www.aamc.org/data-reports/workforce/data/figure-15-percentage-full-time-us-medical-school-faculty-race/ethnicity-2018

15. Hoffman, K. M., Trawalter, S., Axt, J. R., & Oliver, M. B. (2016). Racial bias in facial recognition software and its impact on the accuracy of commercial algorithms. *Proceedings of the National Academy of Sciences of the United States of America, 113*(10), 2765–2772. https://doi.org/10.1073/pnas.1607582113. This was depicted beautifully in a scene from the TV show *The Pitt*. In it, paramedics push a gurney carrying a Black woman, who is thrashing and screaming, into the Emergency Department. As they transfer her to the care of the doctors on the floor, the paramedics dismissively note that she is likely seeking drugs. It's not until another doctor, who trained specifically with a focus on sickle cell anemia, enters the scene that the Black woman is listened to, is treated with dignity, and receives the adequate care that she needs to quell her sickle cell flare.

16. Name has been changed.

17. Merriam-Webster. (n.d.). Racism. In Merriam-Webster.com dictionary. Retrieved July 24, 2025, from https://www.merriam-webster.com/dictionary/racism. In May 2020, a story came out about a young Black woman, Kennedy Mitchum, who took Merriam-Webster to task for their incomplete definition of "racism." Kennedy had experienced many interactions like the one described here, where White people would leverage the dictionary definition of "racism" to discredit her perspective on its more systemic nature. Though it is unclear if or when a change happened, it's worth noting that the Merriam-Webster definition also

includes a definition of racism as "the systemic oppression of a racial group to the social, economic, and political advantage of another."

18. Badger, E., Cain Miller, C., Pearce, A., & Quealy, K. (2018, March 19). Extensive data shows punishing reach of racism for black boys. *New York Times*. https://www.nytimes.com/interactive/2018/03/19/upshot/race-class-white-and-black-men.html

19. Chetty, R., Hendren, N., Kline, P., & Saez, E. (2018). The effects of racial segregation on intergenerational mobility: The case of the United States. Equality of Opportunity Project.

20. Kochhar, R., & Moslimani, M. (2023, December 4). Wealth gaps across racial and ethnic groups. Pew Research Center. https://www.pewresearch.org/2023/12/04/wealth-gaps-across-racial-and-ethnic-groups/

21. McIntosh, P. (1989). White privilege: Unpacking the invisible knapsack. *Peace and Freedom, 49*(4), 10–12.

22. Phillips, L. T., & Lowery, B. S. (2015). The hard-knock life? Whites claim hardships in response to racial inequity. *Journal of Experimental Social Psychology, 61,* 12.

23. Phillips & Lowery, 2015.

24. As with everything, there are nuances to consider. Every White person benefits from White privilege, *and* there are plenty of White individuals who have experienced all kinds of challenges and hardship. This is where the framing of privilege as an inoculator against the worst outcomes is helpful. Even if a White person experiences personal hardship, the evidence is clear that if a person of color were to experience that same personal hardship, the impact would be exponentially worse. Even in the case of people of color who triumph, it's important to consider the headwinds they faced that their White peers would not—and did not—experience.

25. Mendelson, S. (2018, January 25). Octavia Spencer: "Jessica Chastain helped me earn five times my asking salary." BBC News. https://www.bbc.co.uk/news/entertainment-arts-42819003

Chapter 6: Decentering Whiteness

1. Harvard University. (2016, February 2). *Report of the Committee to Study the Importance of Student Body Diversity.* https://inclusionandbelonging taskforce.harvard.edu/files/inclusion/files/report_of_the_committee _to_study_the_importance_of_student_body_diversity_02-02-16.pdf

Notes

2. O'Reilly III, C. A., Williams, K. Y., & Barsade, S. (1998). Group demography and innovation: Does diversity help? In D. H. Gruenfeld (Ed.), *Composition* (pp. 183–207). Elsevier Science/JAI Press; Roberge, M. É., & Van Dick, R. (2010). Recognizing the benefits of diversity: When and how does diversity increase group performance? *Human Resource Management Review*, *20*(4), 295–308; Sommers, S. R. (2006). On racial diversity and group decision making: Identifying multiple effects of racial composition on jury deliberations. *Journal of Personality and Social Psychology*, *90*(4), 597–612. https://doi .org/10.1037/0022-3514.90.4.597; Sommers, S. R. (2008). Beyond information exchange: New perspectives on the benefits of racial diversity for group performance. In K. W. Phillips (Ed.), *Diversity and groups* (vol. 11, pp. 195–220). Emerald Group Publishing. https://doi .org/10.1016/S1534-0856(08)11009-X

3. Phillips, K. W., Northcraft, G. B., & Neale, M. A. (2006). Surface-level diversity and decision-making in groups: When does deep-level similarity help? *Group Processes & Intergroup Relations*, *9*(4), 467–482.

4. Harrison, D. A., Price, K. H., & Bell, M. P. (1998). Beyond relational demography: Time and the effects of surface- and deep-level diversity on work group cohesion. *Academy of Management Journal*, *41*(1), 96–107; Phillips, K. W., Mannix, E. A., Neale, M. A., & Gruenfeld, D. H. (2004). Diverse groups and information sharing: The effects of congruent ties. *Journal of Experimental Social Psychology*, *40*(4), 497–510; Watson, W. E., Kumar, K., & Michaelsen, L. K. (1993). Cultural diversity's impact on interaction process and performance: Comparing homogeneous and diverse task groups. *Academy of Management Journal*, *36*(3), 590–602.

5. *Scientific American*. (2014, October 1). How diversity empowers science and innovation. https://www.scientificamerican.com/report/how -diversity-empowers-science-and-innovation/

6. Phillips, K. W. (2014, October 1). How diversity makes us smarter. *Scientific American*. https://www.scientificamerican.com/article/how -diversity-makes-us-smarter/

7. Richard, O., McMillan, A., Chadwick, K., & Dwyer, S. (2003). Employing an innovation strategy in racially diverse workforces: Effects on firm performance. *Group & Organization Management*,

28(1), 107–126; Dezsö, C. L., & Ross, D. G. (2012). Does female representation in top management improve firm performance? A panel data investigation. *Strategic Management Journal, 33*(9), 1072–1089; Credit Suisse Research Institute. (2012, July 31). *Gender diversity and corporate performance.* https://www.credit-suisse.com/about-us-news/en /articles/media-releases/42035-201207.html; McKinsey & Company. (2015). *Why diversity matters.* McKinsey & Company. https://www .mckinsey.com/business-functions/organization/our-insights/why -diversity-matters; McKinsey & Company. (2018). *Delivering through diversity.* McKinsey & Company. https://www.mckinsey.com/business -functions/organization/our-insights/delivering-through-diversity; McKinsey & Company. (2020). *Diversity wins: How inclusion matters.* McKinsey & Company. https://www.mckinsey.com/business -functions/organization/our-insights/diversity-wins-how-inclusion -matters; McKinsey & Company. (2023). *Diversity matters even more: The case for holistic impact.* McKinsey & Company. https://www .mckinsey.com/featured-insights/diversity-and-inclusion/diversity -matters-even-more-the-case-for-holistic-impact

8. Although she was a graduate student at the time, Dr. Hurd has since completed her doctorate. Therefore, moving forward I will refer to her with her current honorific.

9. Hurd, K., & Plaut, V. C. (2018). Diversity entitlement: Does diversity-benefits ideology undermine inclusion? *Northwestern University Law Review, 112*(6), 1605–1648. https://scholarlycommons.law .northwestern.edu/nulr/vol112/iss6/12/; Plaut, V. C., Romano, C. A., Hurd, K., & Goldstein, E. (2020). Diversity resistance redux: The nature and implications of dominant group threat for diversity and inclusion. In K. M. Thomas (Ed.), *Diversity resistance in organizations* (pp. 103–122). Routledge.

10. Name has been changed.

11. It's worth noting that I only have Anna's version of this story. While her firsthand account is illuminating, and I have no reason to doubt her interpretation, I simply cannot truly know how her behavior affected others without talking to them. I do not know, for example, how her presence impacted her peers in the workshop. It is entirely possible that her decision to stay in the workshop—even with all the adjustments she

made—had a negative impact on the people of color in that space. Maybe there was a different option she could've taken that would have been better than the choice she made. I will never know if this was the case; yet, I still find Anna's insights and reaction to the situation informative, and worth consideration for other White people who are grappling with similar questions.

12. A brief note to acknowledge that, while rare, it *is* possible to have workplace affinity groups for majority group members, like White people or men. However, while the purpose of affinity groups for minority group members is to provide community and a safe space to connect over shared experiences, the purpose of those majority group spaces *should be* to practice the reeducation and accountability that's required of them in diverse spaces. In my professional career, I've only personally seen one such example of this kind of group, but perhaps that will change as more White people become fully aware of their responsibility in detecting bias, dismantling racism, and creating equitable and inclusive spaces.

13. Although my chapter did not compete in this first iteration of the competition, we proudly took second place in the Chicago competition the following year!

14. Hill, J. (2010, March 1). Winners hurt by corporate bad judgment. ESPN. https://www.espn.com/espn/commentary/news/story?id=4956425

15. Every few years, another iteration of this argument emerges. For example, Walmart faced backlash for their Juneteenth ice cream, drink koozies, and party supplies, released the year after Juneteenth was made a federal holiday in the United States. To some, it smacked of opportunism. They pointed out that Walmart could have commemorated the day in other ways, like featuring products from Black-owned businesses. For others, it was the necessary cost of doing business: If you want the holiday to go mainstream, you have to live with the commercialization of it, just as with everything else. Davies, M. (2022, May 24). Walmart apologizes for Juneteenth ice cream and beer koozies. Eater. https://www .eater.com/23139650/walmart-apologizes-for-juneteenth-ice-cream -beer-koozies; Mendoza, D. (2022, May 24). Walmart pulls Juneteenth ice cream from shelves after criticism. KHOU 11 News. https://www .khou.com/article/news/nation-world/walmart-pulls-back-juneteenth -products/507-f3bba6c5-de86-4625-acc7-8c0677b6aac9

Notes

16. I've had a Post-it note with this title on my desk for years. It may happen one day!

Chapter 7: The Subtle Art of Calling Out Bias

1. Name has been changed.
2. Fischer, P., Krueger, J. I., Greitemeyer, T., Vogrincic, C., Kastenmüller, A., Frey, D.,...& Kainbacher, M. (2011). The bystander-effect: A meta-analytic review on bystander intervention in dangerous and non-dangerous emergencies. *Psychological Bulletin, 137*(4), 517.
3. Czopp, A. M., & Monteith, M. J. (2003). Confronting prejudice (literally): Reactions to confrontations of racial and gender bias. *Personality and Social Psychology Bulletin, 29*(4), 532–544; Eliezer, D., & Major, B. (2012). It's not your fault: The social costs of claiming discrimination on behalf of someone else. *Group Processes & Intergroup Relations, 15*(4), 487–502; Gulker, J. E., Mark, A. Y., & Monteith, M. J. (2013). Confronting prejudice: The who, what, and why of confrontation effectiveness. *Social Influence, 8*(4), 280–293; Rasinski, H. M., & Czopp, A. M. (2010). The effect of target status on witnesses' reactions to confrontations of bias. *Basic and Applied Social Psychology, 32*(1), 8–16.
4. Gervais, S. J., & Hillard, A. L. (2014). Confronting sexism as persuasion: Effects of a confrontation's recipient, source, message, and context. *Journal of Social Issues, 70*(4), 653–667.
5. Dickter, C. L., & Newton, V. A. (2013). To confront or not to confront: Non-targets' evaluations of and responses to racist comments. *Journal of Applied Social Psychology, 43*, E262–E275.
6. Ashburn-Nardo, L., Morris, K. A., & Goodwin, S. A. (2008). The confronting prejudiced responses (CPR) model: Applying CPR in organizations. *Academy of Management Learning & Education, 7*(3), 332–342; Ashburn-Nardo, L., & Karim, M. F. A. (2019). The CPR model: Decisions involved in confronting prejudiced responses. In R. K. Mallett & M. J. Monteith (Eds.), *Confronting prejudice and discrimination* (pp. 29–47). Academic Press.
7. Indeed, unequal power dynamics complicate the confronting narrative. Participants who witnessed a biased remark were less likely to confront the speaker if that person was in a leader role rather than a peer. Despite

Notes

perceiving the comment as equally biased, *regardless* of the speaker's position, people felt less responsible for confronting a boss/supervisor, struggled to determine the appropriate response, and determined that the costs of confronting outweighed the benefits. Together, these concerns attenuated people's confrontation intentions. Ashburn-Nardo, L., Blanchar, J. C., Petersson, J., Morris, K. A., & Goodwin, S. A. (2014). Do you say something when it's your boss? The role of perpetrator power in prejudice confrontation. *Journal of Social Issues, 70*(4), 615–636. There's no perfect answer to the question of whether to call out bias, but Dr. Aneeta Rattan, an expert on confronting bias, has a wonderful article in *Harvard Business Review* providing practical tips. She suggests using questions or asking for clarification to draw attention to their statement and provide a chance for correction, *without* initiating an interpersonally costly back-and-forth argument. She also suggests that a private confrontation may be the better way to go, particularly if you are unsure about how the leader will react. Finally, whenever there are power imbalances in play, don't be afraid to use a third party: Other trusted senior leaders, your mentor(s), or HR can help you navigate the situation and any fallout that may occur as a result. Rattan, A. (2020, December 22). Your boss made a biased remark. Should you confront them? *Harvard Business Review.* https://hbr.org/2020/12/your -boss-made-a-biased-remark-should-you-confront-them

8. Czopp, A. M., Monteith, M. J., & Mark, A. Y. (2006). Standing up for a change: Reducing bias through interpersonal confrontation. *Journal of Personality and Social Psychology, 90*(5), 784.

9. Carter, E. R., & Monteith, M. J. (2016, May). *Investigations in racial bias confrontation experiences* [Conference presentation]. 88th Annual Meeting of the Midwestern Psychological Association, Chicago, IL.

10. Rattan, A., Kroeper, K., Arnett, R., Brown, X., & Murphy, M. (2023). Not such a complainer anymore: Confrontation that signals a growth mindset can attenuate backlash. *Journal of Personality and Social Psychology, 124*(2), 344.

11. In this study, a third of participants also received a confrontation message that included no sentence referencing mindset beliefs. Participant responses in this group more closely matched the responses of those in the fixed-mindset confrontation group.

Notes

12. Even worse, the condescending language could backfire entirely. Take, for example, Hillary Clinton's infamous "basket of deplorables" comment, in reference to supporters of then candidate Donald Trump. Instead of becoming remorseful of the idea that their support of Trump was, indeed, deplorable, his supporters galvanized around the phrase, adopted the identity with pride, and doubled down on their beliefs. The social psychologist in me certainly wonders whether a more growth-mindset approach would have yielded different results.

13. Li, W. H. C., Ho, K. Y., Wang, M. P., Cheung, D. Y. T., Lam, K. K. W., Xia, W.,... & Lam, T. H. (2020). Effectiveness of a brief self-determination theory–based smoking cessation intervention for smokers at emergency departments in Hong Kong: A randomized clinical trial. *JAMA Internal Medicine, 180*(2), 206–214; Williams, G. C., McGregor, H. A., Sharp, D., Levesque, C., Kouides, R. W., Ryan, R. M., & Deci, E. L. (2006). Testing a self-determination theory intervention for motivating tobacco cessation: Supporting autonomy and competence in a clinical trial. *Health Psychology, 25*(1), 91; Teixeira, P. J., Carraça, E. V., Markland, D., Silva, M. N., & Ryan, R. M. (2012). Exercise, physical activity, and self-determination theory: A systematic review. *International Journal of Behavioral Nutrition and Physical Activity, 9*, 1–30; Guay, F. (2022). Applying self-determination theory to education: Regulations types, psychological needs, and autonomy supporting behaviors. *Canadian Journal of School Psychology, 37*(1), 75–92.

14. Legault, L., Gutsell, J. N., & Inzlicht, M. (2011). Ironic effects of antiprejudice messages: How motivational interventions can reduce (but also increase) prejudice. *Psychological Science, 22*(12), 1472–1477.

15. It's worth noting that I did *none* of these things in my response to Tracy. I called her homophobic—a label that certainly conveyed a fixed mindset; I pointed out her double standard, which was just a fancy way of calling her incompetent; and I told her that I did not agree with her stance, which, while true, didn't exactly engender a sense of connectedness. I'm thankful that my approach has evolved for the better as I've had more practice with these kinds of situations.

16. BBC News. (2016, June 29). The humble safety pin makes an anti-racism point. BBC News. https://www.bbc.com/news/uk-36661097

Notes

17. Two ribbon trends were prevalent in the 1990s: red ribbons for AIDS awareness and pink ribbons for breast cancer awareness. McDonnell, T. E., Jonason, A., & Christoffersen, K. (2017). Seeing red and wearing pink: Trajectories of cultural power in the AIDS and breast cancer ribbons. *Poetics, 60,* 1–15.

18. These indicators reference the following movements: #StopAsianHate to combat the uptick in anti-Asian hate crimes and bias after the onset of the COVID-19 pandemic; "Black Out Tuesday" to protest anti-Black racism and policy brutality; the Ukrainian flag to show support for Ukraine in the Ukraine-Russia war; and the watermelon (whose colors are the same as the Palestinian flag) to show support for Palestine's autonomy.

19. Defined in Merriam-Webster as "the practice of conspicuously showing support for a cause (as by posting on social media or hanging a flag or sign) without taking any real steps to effect change." Merriam-Webster. (n.d.). Slacktivism. In Merriam-Webster.com dictionary. Retrieved July 25, 2025, from https://www.merriam-webster.com/dictionary /slacktivism; Abad-Santos, A. (2016, November 17). The backlash over safety pins and allies, explained. Vox. https://www.vox.com/culture /2016/11/17/13636156/safety-pins-backlash-trump-brexit

20. Ajzen, I. (1991). The theory of planned behavior. *Organizational Behavior and Human Decision Processes, 50*(2), 179–211; Kan, M. P., & Fabrigar, L. R. (2020). Theory of planned behavior. In V. Zeigler-Hill and T. K. Shackelford (Eds.), *Encyclopedia of personality and individual differences* (pp. 5476–5483). Springer International Publishing.

21. This is definitely how I feel when I look back on my Human Rights Campaign Facebook picture days. As I've engaged more in activism supporting trans folks, I've learned that the Human Rights Campaign has faced criticism for the lack of meaningful support of the trans community. In the years since, I've taken different, and more meaningful, approaches to trans allyship. My own growth in this area gives me a lot of empathy for those who jumped on the safety pin bandwagon years ago.

Chapter 8: Equipping Children to Detect and Challenge Racial Bias

1. As an example, a 2010 report from Pew Research Center declared that Millennials were on track to be the most educated generation

Notes

in American history. However, a report from the same entity nearly a decade later declared that Gen Z now holds that title. Pew Research Center. (2010, February 24). *Millennials: Confident. Connected. Open to change.* Pew Research Center. https://www.pewresearch.org/social-trends/2010/02/24/millennials-confident-connected-open-to-change/; Parker, K., Graf, N., & Igielnik, R. (2019, January 17). *Generation Z looks a lot like Millennials on key social and political issues.* Pew Research Center. https://www.pewresearch.org/social-trends/2019/01/17/generation-z-looks-a-lot-like-millennials-on-key-social-and-political-issues/

2. Edgcumbe, D. R. (2022). Age differences in open-mindedness: From 18 to 87 years of age. *Experimental Aging Research, 48*(1), 24–41. https://doi.org/10.1080/0361073X.2021.1923330

3. Maniam, S., & Smith, S. (2017, March 20). A wider partisan and ideological gap between younger, older generations. Pew Research Center. https://www.pewresearch.org/short-reads/2017/03/20/a-wider-partisan-and-ideological-gap-between-younger-older-generations/

4. Hais, M., & Winograd, M. (2008, December 18). It's official: Millennials realigned American politics in 2008. *HuffPost.* https://www.huffpost.com/entry/its-official-millennials_b_144357

5. Clement, S. (2015, June 23). Millennials are just as racist as their parents. *Washington Post.* https://www.washingtonpost.com/news/wonk/wp/2015/06/23/millennials-are-just-as-racist-as-their-parents/

6. Gaddis, S. M., & Ghoshal, R. (2020). Searching for a roommate: A correspondence audit examining racial/ethnic and immigrant discrimination among millennials. *Socius, 6,* 2378023120972287.

7. Parker, Graf, & Igielnik, 2019.

8. Kayembe, B. (2021, June 16). Gen Z isn't as anti-racist as you think. Vice. https://www.vice.com/en/article/gen-z-isnt-as-anti-racist-as-you-think/

9. Sherman, C. (2024, November 8). "A big cratering": An expert on Gen Z's surprise votes—and young women's growing support for Trump. *The Guardian.* https://www.theguardian.com/us-news/2024/nov/08/young-voters-trump-gen-z

10. Hailey, S. E., & Olson, K. R. (2013). A social psychologist's guide to the development of racial attitudes. *Social and Personality Psychology Compass, 7*(7), 457–469.

Notes

11. Studies testing babies' attention use a "preferential looking paradigm" to surmise preferences, such that longer gaze times at a face or image indicate a stronger preference. Bar-Haim, Y., Ziv, T., Lamy, D., & Hodes, R. M. (2006). Nature and nurture in own-race face processing. *Psychological Science, 17*(2), 159–163.

12. Name has been changed.

13. Aboud, F. E. (2003). The formation of in-group favoritism and out-group prejudice in young children: Are they distinct attitudes? *Developmental Psychology, 39*(1), 48–60. https://doi.org/10.1037/0012-1649.39.1.48; Aboud, F. E., & Amato, M. (2001). Developmental and socialization influences on intergroup bias. In R. Brown & S. Gaertner (Eds.), *Blackwell handbook of social psychology: Intergroup processes* (pp. 65–85). Blackwell Publishers; Cristol, D., & Gimbert, B. (2008). Racial perceptions of young children: A review of literature post-1999. *Early Childhood Education Journal, 36*, 201–207; Kinzler, K. D., & Spelke, E. S. (2011). Do infants show social preferences for people differing in race? *Cognition, 119*(1), 1–9. https://doi.org/10.1016/j.cognition.2010.10.019

14. Griffiths, R., & Nesdale, D. (2006). The role of group norms in predicting adolescents' outgroup attitudes. *International Journal of Intercultural Relations, 30*(6), 693–707. https://doi.org/10.1016/j.ijintrel.2006.06.001; Kowalski, K., & Lo, Y. F. (2001). The influence of perceptual features, ethnic labels, and sociocultural information on the development of ethnic/racial bias in young children. *Journal of Cross-Cultural Psychology, 32*(4), 444–455; Mandalaywala, T. M., Benitez, A., Sagar, D., & Rhodes, M. (2021). The development of intergroup attitudes: The role of group norms and group identity. *Child Development, 92*(3), 1005–1021. https://doi.org/10.1111/cdev.13428; Newheiser, A. K., & Olson, K. R. (2012). The development of racial bias in childhood and adolescence. *Developmental Science, 15*(4), 499–511. https://doi.org/10.1111/j.1467-7637.2012.01198.x

15. Vittrup, B., & Holden, G. W. (2011). Exploring the impact of educational television and parent–child discussions on children's racial attitudes. *Analyses of Social Issues and Public Policy, 11*(1), 82–104.

16. Rogers, L. O., Scott, K. E., Wintz, F., Eisenman, S. R., Dorsi, C., Chae, D., & Meltzoff, A. N. (2024). Exploring whether and how

Notes

Black and White parents talk with their children about race: M(ai)cro race conversations about Black Lives Matter. *Developmental Psychology, 60*(3), 407; Umaña-Taylor, A. J., & Hill, N. E. (2020). Ethnic–racial socialization in the family: A decade's advance on precursors and outcomes. *Journal of Marriage and Family, 82*(1), 244–271; Wang, M. T., Henry, D. A., Smith, L. V., Huguley, J. P., & Guo, J. (2020). Parental ethnic-racial socialization practices and children of color's psychosocial and behavioral adjustment: A systematic review and meta-analysis. *American Psychologist, 75*(1), 1.

17. Olson, K. R., Shutts, K., Kinzler, K. D., & Weisman, K. (2012). Children's social preferences and the development of intergroup attitudes. *Developmental Psychology, 48*(5), 1371–1381. https://doi.org/10.1037/a0027487; Shutts, K., Brey, E. L., Dornbusch, L. A., Slywotzky, N., & Olson, K. R. (2016). Children use wealth cues to evaluate others. *PLOS One, 11*(3), e0149360. https://doi.org/10.1371/journal.pone.0149360; Sullivan, J., Wilton, L., & Apfelbaum, E. P. (2021). Adults delay conversations about race because they underestimate children's processing of race. *Journal of Experimental Psychology: General, 150*(2), 395.

18. Newheiser, A. K., Dunham, Y., Merrill, A., Hoosain, L., & Olson, K. R. (2014). Preference for high status predicts implicit outgroup bias among children from low-status groups. *Developmental Psychology, 50*(4), 1081.

19. Centre for Literacy in Primary Education. (2020). *Reflecting realities: Survey of ethnic representation within UK children's literature 2019.* https://clpe.org.uk/system/files/CLPE%20Reflecting%20Realities%202020.pdf

20. Room to Read. (2021, August 30). *Room to Read investigates scarcity of books and lack of book diversity for children in the U.S.* https://www.roomtoread.org/the-latest/room-to-read-investigates-scarcity-of-books-and-lack-of-book-diversity-for-children-in-the-us/

21. Abaied, J. L., & Perry, S. P. (2021). Socialization of racial ideology by White parents. *Cultural Diversity & Ethnic Minority Psychology, 27*(3), 431.

22. Samaria Rice, Tamir's mother, has leaned into advocacy in the years following her son's murder to equip parents and children with this kind

of information. In 2019, she partnered with the ACLU of Ohio to create a safety handbook instructing youth on how to handle encounters with law enforcement (*Tamir Rice Safety Handbook,* https://www.acluohio.org /en/tamir-rice-safety-handbook).

23. Emerson, L. M., Ogielda, C.. & Rowse, G. (2019). The role of experiential avoidance and parental control in the association between parent and child anxiety. *Frontiers in Psychology, 10,* 262.

24. Perry, S., Skinner, A. L., Abaied, J. L., Osnaya, A., & Waters, S. (2020, May 18). Initial evidence that parent-child conversations about race reduce racial biases among White U.S. children. https://doi .org/10.31234/osf.io/3xdg8

25. If you're reading this and this has happened to you, you know exactly what I'm talking about. And if you're reading this and it *hasn't* happened to you, just wait. Maybe it won't be a comment about race, but your child *will* wonder aloud why someone is walking with a cane or other mobility-assisting device, or sternly declare to your gender-nonconforming friend that girls are supposed to wear dresses (the latter of which *absolutely* happened while a child was under my care).

26. Grusec, J. E. (2023). Moral development from a socialization perspective. In M. Killen & J. G. Smetana (Eds.), *Handbook of moral development* (3rd ed., pp. 323–338). Routledge; Smetana, J. G., Jambon, M., & Ball, C. (2014). The social domain approach to children's moral and social judgments. In M. Killen & J. G. Smetana (Eds.), *Handbook of moral development* (2nd ed., pp. 23–45). Psychology Press.

Conclusion: A Case for Optimism and a Final Call to Action

1. Fortune. (2021, November 30–December 1). Fortune Brainstorm Tech 2021 agenda. Fortune. https://fortune.com/conferences/fortune -brainstorm-tech-2021/agenda

2. McGirt, E., & Vanian, J. (2021, December 17). There is still reason to be optimistic about race and corporate diversity. *Fortune.* https:// fortune.com/2021/12/17/optimism-race-corporate-diversity-dei -evelyn-carter-paradigm/

3. Per the King Institute at Stanford University, the earliest known use of the title comes from King's 1959 commencement address at Morehouse

Notes

College. King made edits and adjustments to this speech over the years, and while the quote mentioned here is not in that original version, it is present in the 1965 version of the speech, delivered at Oberlin College, as well as the address at the National Cathedral in 1968. King, M. L., Jr. (1965, June). "Remaining awake through a great revolution" [Commencement address, Oberlin College]. In *Martin Luther King, Jr. at Oberlin*. Oberlin College Archives. Retrieved from https://www2.oberlin.edu/external /EOG/BlackHistoryMonth/MLK/CommAddress.html

4. Charlesworth, T. E., & Banaji, M. R. (2019). The influence of implicit racial attitudes on evaluation and behavior. *Current Opinion in Psychology, 32*, 101–106. https://doi.org/10.1016/j.copsyc.2019.06.014; Mazumder, S. (2018). The persistent effect of US civil rights protests on political attitudes. *American Journal of Political Science, 62*(4), 922–935.

Index

affirmative action
  Bakke case and, 135–137
  diversity and, 140, 146
  in higher education, 72
  in hiring process, 68
allyship
  conversations with children
    about, 215
  symbols used for, 184–190,
    259n17, 259n18, 259n19,
    259n21
  workshops on, 41–44, 46,
    50–51, 151
America
  as "melting pot," 91, 246n11
  redemptive story of, 16
  Whiteness associated with, 89,
    245n8
amygdala, 35
Andersen, Hans Christian,
  247n20
Anderson, Carol, 107
antibias education, 17
anti-Black bias, 36–38, 72, 99, 114,
  182. *See also* racial bias

anti-racism education, 101, 102
anti-racism workshops, 157
anti-White bias, 99. *See also*
  racial bias
"anti-woke" pundits, 78
Asian people
  complainer effect and, 70
  race/ethnicity indicators on
    résumés, 68
  religious and cultural observances
    of, 105–106
Association of American Medical
  Colleges, 120
awareness gaps
  body size and, 97–98, 103
  minding of, 15–17, 81

Bailey, Halle, 98
Bakke, Allan, 136
banned books, 228
behaviors, modeling of, 25–26
being competent, 14–15
being liked, 14–15
bias. *See also* racial bias; systemic
  racism

Index

bias *(cont.)*
  acknowledgment of, 28,
    29–30, 54
  awareness of, 4, 10
  evidence-based approaches to
    combating, 10
  fixed mindset and, 66, 180,
    257n11
  growth mindset and, 18–23, 30,
    54, 163, 179–180
  identification of, 5, 179
  implicit bias, 7, 115
  inference studies on, 172–174,
    179–180
  intention versus impact and,
    63, 66
  interpersonal expressions of, 117
  intrinsic motivation and, 48–50
  malleability of, 23
  research studies on, 19, 21–22,
    238n11
  scale of problem, 6
  systemic expressions of, 117
  unconscious expressions of, 7,
    19–20, 39–40, 47–48, 50,
    123, 148
  understanding nuances of, 15
bias confrontation
  agency and autonomy emphasized
    in, 181–183
  bystander effect and, 168
  challenges of, 177–178
  consequences of, 176–177
  cost-benefit analysis of, 171, 177
  fixed mindset language and,
    258n15
  garden analogy for, 190–191
  growth-mindset language and,
    179–181, 183, 258n12

  importance of, 178
  interconnectedness emphasized
    in, 183–184
  interpersonal risks of, 180–181,
    258n12
  as interruption of harmful
    behavior, 172
  meaningful change created by,
    171–172, 175
  phrasing choices for, 170–171,
    172, 172–174, 175, 182–183
  power dynamics of, 171, 178,
    256–257n7
  preservation of relationship and,
    178–179
  prior experiences shaping, 171
  public confrontation of, 169
  public declarations and, 184–191
  reluctance to speak up, 167,
    168–169, 170, 175
  research on, 169–170,
    172–176, 179
  vulnerability and, 183–184
  whether to confront, 167–168,
    170–171, 174–175
  White people's excuses for biased
    statements, 9
bias detection
  accuracy in, 65
  anti-White bias and, 75
  cognitive cost of, 63–65
  early warning signs of, 74
  gaps in, 3, 4, 6, 14–15
  growth mindset and, 14, 25,
    163
  hypervigilance and, 65
  intrinsic motivation and, 48
  as learned skill, 5, 6, 8, 14, 28,
    30–31, 60, 69, 72, 74, 218

266

Index

microaggressions and, 65–67,
  241n7
as nuanced art, 17
subtle forms of bias and, 63–65,
  69, 74
White privilege and, 108
Black Lives Matter, 63, 187
Black people
  best places to live lists and, 85
  bias experienced by, 80
  complainer effect and, 71–72,
    242–243n14
  "discomfort/unfamiliarity with,"
    62, 65–67
  diversity's effects on, 144
  friction experienced by, 86
  medical research on, 119
  N-word and, 160
  race/ethnicity indicators on
    résumés, 68
  racial bias perceived by, 99–100
  racial wealth gap and, 125
  racism defined by, 61
  research on lived experience
    of, 75
Black women
  birth team for, 111
  doctors' attitudes toward, 110
  maternal mortality rate of,
    112, 113
  pregnancy and birthing risks of,
    109–114, 249n3
  systemic racism within maternal
    healthcare and, 126
  uterine fibroids and, 120
body language, as unconscious
  expression of bias, 19
body size, air travel experiences and,
  97–98, 103, 246–247n15

book bans, 102
Brexit, 184, 185–186, 187
Brown, Michael, 212
Brown v. Board of Education
  (1954), 138
bystander effect, 168

California, Texas social studies
  textbooks compared to, 16–17
California Supreme Court, 136
call to action, 229–230
Carr, Priyanka, 18, 20–21
Carter, Evelyn R.
  advanced math classes and, 23–24
  air travel experiences of, 96–97
  as Black woman growing up in
    White environments, 3, 39,
    58–59, 60, 84–85
  childhood perception of racism,
    200–201, 213
  as DEI professional, 3–4, 39–44,
    50–52, 65–66, 92–96, 121,
    122–123, 126, 131, 132,
    141, 144, 146–148, 153–155,
    225–226
  hair care and, 58–59, 60, 81, 84, 86
  hiring research assistant, 28–31
  mother of, 11, 33–35, 47, 248n29
  at Paradigm, 147
  pregnancy of, 112–114, 126
  racial biases of, 7
  research career of, 78–79, 145,
    167, 170, 171–172, 178
  sorority of, 161
  violin skills developed by, 11–13
  Washington, DC, trip of, 57–59,
    240n1
  zip-lining experience of, 33–35,
    46–47, 53, 54

267

Index

Center for Racial Justice in Education, 224
Chang, Jade, 107
Charles, Ray, 159
Charleston church shooting, 212
Chastain, Jessica, 130–131
children
  awareness of racial differences and, 206, 208
  bias addressed in, 191, 198
  bias learned from environment, 201–203
  book selection for, 208–211, 224
  color-conscious approach and, 205–207, 208
  conversations about race and racism, 212–217
  correcting biases through words and actions, 219–223, 263n25
  differences perceived by, 199–200, 206–207, 220–221
  diverse media exposure and, 208–212, 221
  fear of imperfect race-related discussions with, 217–219
  limited exposure to different races, 201
  parents' growth shaped by, 223
  preferential looking pattern and, 199–200, 261n11
  race-related conversations with, 203–204, 223
  racial perception developed in, 199–204
  refreshing presence of, 193
  reinforcing sense of agency, 217
  resources to support education about race and racism, 224
  as sources of possibility, 194

TV show and movie selection for, 211, 221
children's literature, 26
cities
  best places to live for Black people, 85
  best places to live lists for White people, 83–86, 244n2
  racial representation in, 83–84, 244n3, 244n4, 245n6
Clinton, Hillary, 70, 258n12
code-switching, 153
color blindness
  challenging of, 108
  color consciousness as contrast to, 205–207
  myth of, 89–92, 246n11
color consciousness, 205–207, 208
communication, disrupting norms of, 164
community
  accountability for learning, 26–27
  growth mindset and, 12, 24, 25, 27
competence, as fundamental human need, 14, 15
Confederate flag, 63
Confronting Bias workshops, 174–175
criminal justice system, 124–125
cultural appropriation, 161–162, 255n15
curiosity, 207

defensiveness, 39, 49
DEI (diversity, equity, and inclusion)
  conversations about, 18

Index

Index

..

Index

Index

racial bias *(cont.)*
  overt expressions of, 63–64, 76
  in pay and promotion, 68
  people of color's experiences of, 5, 15, 60, 71, 77, 78, 79–81, 88, 156
  people of color's perception of, 3, 6, 61, 63, 100
  perceptions of, 3, 6
  persistence across generations, 196–198, 223
  prevalence of, 4, 7
  racism compared to, 8
  reduction in, 6
  roots of, 4
  Stroop task and, 37–38
  subtle expressions of, 9, 61, 63–65, 73–76, 77, 78
  understanding of, 15–16
  White people's advantages and, 88
  White people's experience of, 74–78
  White people's perception of, 3, 4–5, 6, 8, 15–16, 60, 61, 62–63, 73–76, 80, 81, 99–100, 243–244n23
racial discrimination, 4, 7, 69, 70
racial dynamics, awareness of, 16
racial equality, progress toward, 99, 101–102
racial equity
  becoming champion for, 6
  discussions about, 157
  extrinsic motivation and, 52–53
  historical and present inequities, 15
  interventions and, 44–45
  intrinsic motivation and, 52

  Barack Obama's presidency and, 102
  progress toward, 3–4, 10
  racial bias as undermining factor, 15
  societal functioning and, 5
  support for, 129, 130, 156
  White people as beneficiaries of, 150
  White people lashing out against, 98–99
racial hierarchies, 146, 201
racial identities
  conversations about, 108
  naming of, 92
  preference for status quo and, 99, 101, 102, 104
  Whiteness as racial identity, 9, 81, 92–96, 108, 114, 127, 246n14
racial justice, 129, 187, 216, 227–230
racial privilege. *See also* White privilege
  awareness of, 104, 127–129
racial progress
  changes in status quo and, 100, 101, 102
  impediments to, 5
  population changes and, 102
  reversal of, 4, 227
racial reckoning, 44
racial wealth gap, 125
racism. *See also* systemic racism
  Black people's defining of, 61
  children's exposure to, 202
  common misperceptions of, 9, 17, 121–122
  as constant threat for people of color, 15

Index

Students for Fair Admissions v. Harvard (2023), 137
Students for Fair Admissions v. University of North Carolina (2023), 137
success
  meritocratic view of, 68
  standards for, 64
Sundance Film Festival, 130
systemic racism
  affirmative action practices and, 136–137
  awareness of, 9, 113–114, 121–122, 126–127, 132–133
  compounding impact of, 121–127
  conversations about, 18
  definition of, 251–252n17
  diversity initiatives' reinforcement of, 143
  in healthcare system, 113–114, 117–120, 125, 126, 251n15
  individual decisions and, 130
  layers of, 117–120
  patterns of, 116
  perpetuation of, 9
  societal impacts of, 18
  studies of, 125
  White experiences prioritized by, 116–117, 150

teenagers
  conversations about race and racism, 216
  resources for, 224
Texas, California social studies textbooks compared to, 16–17
"Think Before You Speak" public service announcements, 18

Trump, Donald, 70–71, 102, 184, 186, 197, 240n3, 258n12
Tumblr, 71–72

unconscious bias, 7, 19–20, 39–40, 47–48, 50, 123, 148
underrepresentation, experience of, 79–80
U.S. Supreme Court, 136–137, 146
university campuses, diversity of, 85, 245n5
University of California, Davis, 136

values
  aligning behavior with, 49, 53–54
  conversations with children about race and, 215
  symbolic expression of, 184–190, 259n17, 259n18, 259n19, 259n21
violin practice, 11–13
virtue signaling, 184–191
vulnerability
  in approach to bias, 10
  bias confrontation and, 183–184
  in expression of values, 185
  growth mindset and, 24, 25
  in White spaces, 151

We Need Diverse Books, 224
West, Keon, 78
White children
  conversations about race and racism, 212–217
  in-group favoritism of, 201–202
  learning process about race, 199–205
White culture, White default and, 88, 89, 117, 154

Index

Whiteness
  decentering of, 151–164
  hierarchy prioritizing of, 8, 9, 15,
    88–89, 92, 108
  off-limits cultural spaces and,
    159–164
  preservation of White default,
    100–101
  psychology of White default,
    96–102
  as racial identity, 9, 81, 92–96,
    108, 114, 127, 246n14
  redemptive story of, 16
  as unspoken default, 9, 59,
    81, 87–89, 92, 95–96, 104,
    106–107, 135, 210, 245n8
  White spaces and, 39,
    151–158, 164
White people
  affirmative action violating rights
    of, 136
  anti-White bias experienced by,
    74–78
  attunement to identification of
    bias, 5–6
  awareness gap and, 15–16, 81
  awareness of racial bias and, 47
  best places to live lists and, 83–87
  bias definition and, 61, 62–63
  bias detection skills and, 5, 6, 69,
    72, 74
  commitment to combating racial
    bias, 229–230
  DEI initiatives and, 39–43,
    147–148
  diversity's benefit for, 142, 143,
    144, 145, 146–147, 149, 150
  entitlement of, 163
  fear of being "found out," 8

growth mindset about bias and,
  18–19
growth mindset about racial bias
  and, 23
hierarchy prioritizing Whiteness
  and, 8, 9, 15
homogenous friend groups of,
  102–103, 106, 248n24
homogenous networks of, 122
individualism afforded to, 29
interracial interactions and,
  20–23, 36–39, 45
misconceptions about race and
  racism, 9, 61–62, 70–71,
  121–122
N-word and, 160–161
ongoing learning process on
  racism, 23–24
psychological barriers of, 8–9
racial bias directed at, 74
racial bias experienced by,
  74–78
racial bias perceived by, 3, 4–5, 6,
  8, 15–16, 60, 61, 62–63, 73–76,
  80, 81, 99–100, 243–244n23
racial harm acknowledged by, 5
racial identity of, 9, 81, 92–96,
  108, 114, 127
racial wealth gap and, 125
racism defined by, 61–62, 63,
  73, 121
as reference point in diversity
  studies, 142–143, 144
reverse racism experiences of, 75
talking about racial bias and,
  35–36
Whiteness as unspoken default
  and, 9, 59, 81, 87–89, 92,
  122–123, 151–153, 154

Index

About the Author

Evelyn R. Carter, PhD, is a social psychologist and an author of cutting-edge research on how to detect and discuss racial bias. As a diversity, equity, and inclusion expert, she has applied these evidence-based practices to a vast array of industries, from higher education to financial services, technology, retail, and professional sports, and at organizations and institutions such as American Express, Burberry, Cushman & Wakefield, Nike, the NFL, Uber, and UCLA. Known for blending research, pop culture, and corporate DEI practices into unique insights, Dr. Carter has been featured in *The Atlantic*, *USA Today*, Bloomberg, *CBS This Morning*, CNBC, *Fast Company*, *Harvard Business Review*, and NPR.

RAISING READERS
Books Build Bright Futures

Thank you for reading this book and for being a reader of books in general. We are so grateful to share being part of a community of readers with you, and we hope you will join us in passing our love of books on to the next generation of readers.

Did you know that reading for enjoyment is the single biggest predictor of a child's future happiness and success?

More than family circumstances, parents' educational background, or income, reading impacts a child's future academic performance, emotional well-being, communication skills, economic security, ambition, and happiness.

Studies show that kids reading for enjoyment in the US is in rapid decline:

- In 2012, 53% of 9-year-olds read almost every day. Just 10 years later, in 2022, the number had fallen to 39%.
- In 2012, 27% of 13-year-olds read for fun daily. By 2023, that number was just 14%.

Together, we can commit to **Raising Readers** and change this trend. How?

- Read to children in your life daily.
- Model reading as a fun activity.
- Reduce screen time.
- Start a family, school, or community book club.
- Visit bookstores and libraries regularly.
- Listen to audiobooks.
- Read the book before you see the movie.
- Encourage your child to read aloud to a pet or stuffed animal.
- Give books as gifts.
- Donate books to families and communities in need.

BOB1217

Books build bright futures, and **Raising Readers** is our shared responsibility.

For more information, visit **JoinRaisingReaders.com**

Sources: National Endowment for the Arts, National Assessment of Educational Progress, WorldBookDay.com, Nielsen BookData's 2023 "Understanding the Children's Book Consumer"